JOBS WITH
ZERO-CAPITAL
(vol.one)

Jobs With
ZERO-CAPITAL
(vol.one)

EXPLICIT. MOTIVATIONAL. PRACTICABLE.
TOWARDS BEING MY OWN BOSS.

AMUSA ABDULATEEF

authorHOUSE®

AuthorHouse™
1663 Liberty Drive
Bloomington, IN 47403
www.authorhouse.com
Phone: 1-800-839-8640

Published by AuthorHouse   04/25/2012

ISBN: 978-1-4685-0374-6 (sc)
ISBN: 978-1-4685-0373-9 (hc)
ISBN: 978-1-4685-0375-3 (e)

CONTENTS

Part Two

PREFACE

First and foremost, **I congratulate you** for picking this work of research on **jobs** creation. It is the antidote to the scourge of unemployment. There is no doubt the fact that a government that does not have enough capital to fix social infrastructures would not be able to provide capital for prospective entrepreneurs to start a good business. Also, individual venture capitalists whose businesses cannot assess loans from financial houses to save their own businesses from collapsing in this era of global credit crunch can never help to turn a dream of a potential self-employed brimming with business ideas into a reality. Lastly, no insolvent banks dare risk providing any start-up capital for new businesses. We must not hence fold our arms to solve the riddle. The adverse effects of the unemployment to our generation are too enormous to ignore. This prompted the research into the starting point—finding such **jobs** the unemployed on the street can start without capital (dosh)! **Jobs** with zero capital remain the best bet for cash—strapped prospective entrepreneurs. The first **jobs** as a worthy bailout on which many businesses worldwide today also took their source!

Assuredly, after reading through, you are no doubt free from being idle as you have all what it takes to add values to other people's lives. Within are different categories of **jobs** of not less than **fifty** which you can start without a penny! The **jobs** have **sub—jobs** running to **hundreds** depending on your creativity and these can provide **jobs** for **millions** across each nation even with the inadequate social infrastructures! Readers would learn to know **how to start,** saving funds **to expand** such business and many other things. You will learn not less than **eight major ways** to get funds to start the zero-capital **jobs.** Relevant quotes and practical life experiences of many successful business moguls are employed. Under each category is poetic form as a summary.

This 'unputdownable' work of research is targeted at the unemployed graduates, the idle youths in particular, wandering the streets in search of employments and the skilled talented ones. It is also meant for those who have **jobs (self-employed)** but are facing the task of getting enough capital to boost the business. **Adding values to lives is creating jobs that enrich lives.** As a sportsman, you create amusement for people to relax; as a technician, you remove the stress from people while repairing their breakdown gadgets . . . . People laud your sacrifices and efforts, no matter how tiny, to give them joy and satisfaction from giving value to their monies. This is **your own joy** as you are the master and controller of your time, brains and skills. This is **the joy of being self-employed.** You are **your own boss** and **dictating the pace as the leader of others!** "The best employment is the earning from one's hands" according to the noblest of creatures. This is no doubt self—employment. **Brian Tracy wrote in his book "Getting rich your own way" that 74% of America millionaires are self-made entrepreneurs (They are self-employed!).** Many multimillionaires in the nation are once self-employed. **They started with nothing or little.** It gives one joy to **start an idea** and from there employ others to **make the idea a reality** as target. It should be echoed to the ears of people that not all graduates and skilled men and women would have the opportunity to work in offices as employees. Some **unemployed** are parasites as some are saprophytes. Some work in synergy (partners/shareholders). For a category of those who are **self-employed,** they determine their gross earnings, overheads and other business expenditures. They determine the time of retirement and how to spend their leisure time. This writer, as **a self-employed,** believes that man needs to work for six months in a year when the weather is friendly and enjoy holiday for the rest. This however depends on the nature of **job** one is doing. A manufacturer who produces for marketers and sellers to sell need not worry at a time if enough products are in warehouse.

He just needs to produce what (the product/service) the consumer would buy at a price based on their disposable income. It is <u>not</u> commercially viable to sell pork and alcohol in Muslims-dominated town/nation. Provide lucrative **jobs** for all the restless idle youths and the insecurity and its huge expenses are put into a halt. The more the **jobs** the more the taxes and investment opportunities in a peaceful atmosphere. Meanwhile, no matter how poor a nation is, there are relevant **jobs** that can thrive there even the drought-prone and natural disaster-prone areas. **Dubai was a desert that has become a hub of investors worldwide!** The founders of modern **Dubai** only transformed the land. Human capital (intellectual resources) can be developed in such nation that would create **jobs** opportunities later. **Japan is a good case study!**

It is amazing seeing people complaining about unemployment in the midst of numerous **jobs** to be done, to this socio-economic research-writer. Skilled graduates should **hone their skills at the right time and right places**. Tell an unemployed graduate on the streets that there are **jobs** for him to do, he will ask 'where?' Whereas **jobs** exist in thousands aside those that can be created from the existing ones through creating something unique. **Unemployment has been one of the Millennium Development Goals as a global problem threatening the existence of mankind.** It is believed that a jobless man cannot meet his basic needs. Singles among would not marry paving way for raping, gangsterism, armed robbery, kidnapping for ransom as in some nations at the moment and illicit and irresponsible social life.

The problem of joblessness among the populace is **the fear to convert their interests, innate talents, inherited jobs and hobbies into real money-earning jobs.** Had people worked to make careers out of them and devote full time, then **jobs** will be in excess for outsiders or the generations unborn. Let an artist start small and move up the ladder, **jobs** will be created in excess for millions and labour market will have to import workers beyond the shores. Graduates and skilled men should not be on look-out for **non-existing jobs.** It is hightime they heeded the admonition of the noblest among us that says **'learn to know yourself'**. Having discovered self, then you can map out strategies to showcase your talents for patronage. Sincerely speaking, your weak points that need solution are with numerous others, if you work on finding lasting solution to them, you would make legitimate money. **This book serves as eyes opener to numerous jobs that can employ the idle youths.** A step further to move up the ladder means that the **jobs** will later employ at least in tens (directly and indirectly).In this book are **one-man jobs,** based on skills and talents, **jobs** that can employ hundreds with good remuneration. This book is written in answer to numerous requests of people the writer had counselled on **job** provision and establishment who ignorantly never aware that there are **jobs** at their beck and call classified as **JOBS ONE CAN START WITHOUT A DIME!** We mean **without a start-up capital.**

By capital, we mean amount needed to acquire office building, equipment and other assets for use. Many things are at the beck and call of most unemployed. These include basic allowances, mobile set and assess to internet facility at cheap and affordable cost. With proper use of them, one can start one's **job** with <u>no capital</u>. Never be afraid, **Billionaire Warren Buffett started too** at thirteen **with NOTHING just as most American multimillionaires in history!** You only need government support through passage of enhancing bills and implementation of consistent policies, thereby creating a business-friendly environ. People are naturally creative in a serene environment.

When we say **a dime,** we really mean **'no penny'** save what you are able to raise from feeding, clothing or transportation allowances from parents or guardians or what you are given as gifts from neighbours for an errand. This is financial discipline and control! Remember **Clement Stone, the penniless paperboy on the street of Chicago amassed over $800 millions!** So, you too can start a **job** or business with zero capital! Just like a honeyed-hole bee-hive attracts bees, to build up a **nest egg**, every naira or a percent saved from your basic expenses is enough attraction to save more if you keep in mind what is at stake (as a running cost/take off 'grant' of the **job** so desired to start).At least, no man can live without a social cost no matter how small. For those who have lost families, charities from individuals, social and religious organizations and a **personal sacrifice to save a bit** from that meagre amount would help them to start with little to get just 'a big note and a biro' for a writer, researcher or a collector for use as materials needed. **Let saving become an art, a discipline and an interest**. Bear it in mind that all inventions and techniques are first documented in prints. Most of the businesses we are going to discuss need to be reduced into writing and typesetting.

For the about to be discussed **jobs,** those who are lazy and do not have the courage to set up and manage their own business cannot value this research-based work aim at solving the global war on unemployment. After reading through the pages, you, millions of unemployed youths and employables even among the people living with disabilities (PWDs) across **Africa, Asia Australia, America and Europe**, open a new page in your life and start a **job** with courage! Never allow fear and failure to get capital to tie you down. This is the reason having this book showing other ways to start different **jobs** without a penny from your pocket. Use some or even all the **eight ways** to generate funds for your business idea as illustrated in this work. Be courageous. Give one of the numerous **jobs** within a shot!

ACKNOWLEDGEMENT

*I acknowledge the Bestower of the inspiration, the **ALMIGHTY GOD** who makes the babe to speak and taught pen what to write for the benefit of mankind. The writer is a pen of the **Creator** for nailing to coffin the social risks from the high rate of unemployment and the spread of poverty across the world. Millions of thanks to **Mr. Babatunde Olajide Yusuf** (Director, **Omics Technology**, Ibadan Nigeria) for his constructive criticisms to make this work a uniquely good piece. My heartfelt appreciation goes to **Hon. Olalekan Kazeem Sanni** (Souvenir Print, Ibadan Nigeria) too. Not forgetting my ever reliable soul mate, ever loving and humane prime minister, **Kudirah Joy nee Oladipupo** for her full support of both home and office. She provides the safety net in the course of producing this work.*

*Worth mentioning are the following people for standing by me through the thick and thin of my life—Mr. B.O. Adebisi and his dear wife Mrs. V.O.A. Adebisi, Mr. Tajudeen Oladipupo, Mr. M. O. Mustapha of **F**orest **R**esearch **I**nstitute of **N**igeria, Mrs. Oluwakemi Monsurah Najim, and numerous others.*

*A lot of thanks, endless appreciation to the chamber of **Barrister E.M. Ayeokutan** for supply of the print media for reviews indirectly; same goes to **Mr. Babatunde Olajide Yusuff** whose yeoman support for the facilities enjoyed in his office that is unquantifiable. I will never forget **Mr. O.O. Adeoti**, former **H**ead **o**f **D**epartment, Business and Public Administration Department, **The Polytechnic, Ibadan, Nigeria**. His lectures and challenge to produce feasibility studies on ten **jobs** nobody has never done in our areas prompted the researching and writing of **NEW JOBS FROM***

EXISTING JOBS. *Some of the* **jobs** *are extracted and re-packaged to write the jobs with zero-capital.*

I equally thank my ex-fellow corper, **Mr. Emeka Uwasomba**, *at the place of my primary assignment at* **D**ay **S**econdary **School**, **Shiroro, Niger State** *of* **Nigeria**. *His worries over the next thing after service and the problem of being self-employed with unavailable capital and the bad management of resources by the government of the day prompted me the more to start working on the solution to self-employed inclined people. The challenge has resulted into this product and the others on* **jobs** *creation under different titles.*

Not forgetting my spiritual friends like Mr. Muhyideen Bukhari, Mr. Mohammed Peace Olakunle (Sasco), Mr. Ali Bilal, Mr. Babatunde Owolabi, Mr. Babatunde Ahmed Sanni, Mr. Quadri Issa, Mr. Alade, Mr. Wasiu Alli-Balogun, Mr. Kassim Jimoh Olufemi, Mr. Abdulateef Akinola Olaniyan and those who worked at every point in time for their irresistible and invaluable advices, suggestions and recommendations in the compilation and typesetting works. They are all great and worthy of mentioning in the roll call of honour. To them all, I doff my hat!

Endless appreciation to the inevitable Godsend <u>broker</u>, **Abdulkabir Oladiti**, *Hardware Engineer with* **Arit of Africa** *and the sponsor of this work,* **Mr. Ganiy Hamid, Consultant, PR Ventures Limited**. *This attitude is enough to prove that you too can start making money from simple* **brokerage service** *and* **adding value to your wealth** *like the duo and the owner of the work is able to establish/commence a business without spending a dime from his purse!*

Not forgetting the contributions and encouragements of **Tony Haris** *and particularly,* **Shane Duff, publishing consultant** *from the* **S**ales *and* **M**arketing **D**epartment *of* **Author House** *for her enthusiasm to get this work done under the label.*

My indebtedness appreciation goes to publishers of **<u>The Punch newspaper</u>, Nigeria, Nigerian Institute of Marketing** *and* **<u>Oxford Advanced Learner Dictionary</u>** *whose publications are helping guides towards going thus far. Thanks the contributions from the great books from* **Brian Tracy** *titled <u>"Getting rich on your own way"</u>,* **Dale Carnegie** *on <u>"How to make more</u>*

friends and influence people", **Tom Sant,** *author of "Persuasive Business Proposals" and* **George Classon's** *"The Richest man in Babylon". The materials make an inevitable references explored in the making of this work.*

I am eternally grateful to my parents (of blessed memory). Also to my ex-teachers, mentors and financiers while at schools—Mr. Bayo Olafusi, Mrs. Tomilayo Laniya (Bloom group of schools), Mrs. Felicia Modupe Adeleke (Proprietress, Nickdel group of schools), Pastor and Mrs. Anike Abe, Alhaji Kunle Sanni, Alhaja Rafat Idowu Kunle Sanni, Mr. Abdulrazak Busari—Olaoye and my dear inestimable friends in need and indeed, Messrs Oseni Jimoh Folayemi (major), Isiaq Ademola Olaoye, Awujoola Olalekan Joel among others numerous to mention.

DEDICATION

Dedicated to millions of unemployed youths striving to be self-employed in my nation, Nigeria, who are firm believers in her survival in spite of the maladministration and the corruption within eating deep into the fabrics of the project-Nigeria('the good people, the great nation')

PROLOGUE

I had a discussion with a friend during the recent fuel subsidy removal crisis in the nation. He bared his mind thus:"Our generation has been wasted already. We are only protesting to save our children's future". I itched to know the reasons. He replied "Most of us protesters running to over sixty millions are over thirty years of age with no **job** in spite of our outstanding qualifications, degrees, diplomas and professional certificates, personal skills, talents and specialisations, to sustain ourselves. Most are still depending hence tied to the aprons of their aged, retired parents for basic needs. Unfortunately, employment age has been pegged to between 24 and 27 in most government ministries and private corporations. The few juicy vacant posts are filled with their own children as nepotism and federal character come into play. Other slots to fill for the limited vacant positions are for sale to those who can afford them. Procurement of employees is mostly done by politically constituted boards and that is the major reason for employing incompetent personnels into government jobs". I nodded in total affirmation. It means we have to be on our own (becoming self employed) to survive if we cannot afford to seek for green pasture outside the shores of the nation. I think that should be the best bet as one can nurse a business for the next generation to take over of later. Afterall, those big businesses started small one day from the idea of one man or a group of likeminds who could be family members or friends. Then, I realised the inevitable and utmost importance of releasing the research manuscripts on **jobs** the unemployment can start developing from zero capital and other titles for the benefit of mankind at all climes. **'A sauce for goose is a sauce for gander'**, the wise saying goes.

"Verily, We have created man into toil and struggle" the light says. Another scripture rightly says: *"No food for a lazy man"*. Generating lucrative employments for the idlers is a major **MDGs** to halt the social risks of the world unemployed populace. Every nation including the developed nations is battling with the scourge of unemployment for the populace. As a result of the economic meltdown across the world, one of the first effects is loss of **jobs** and redundancy particularly in the financial sector, then the cut in take home pay in the month as a result, some 50%; some even more that those with **jobs** are forced to be living far below average. Many families are living **under two dollars per day** (less than fifty cents per head) in a nation reputed to be the giant of the black race in terms of natural and human resources, whose poverty level has risen to **over 75 percent** (where a family is on a dollar per day!) according to the nation's **C**entral **B**ank **G**overnor and **BBC** February 2012 reports respectively. In short, all nations are working to get solutions to the monster called unemployment which has reduced the living standard into abject poverty which leads populace into crimes in all forms. In fact, it has become a major **M**illennium **D**evelopment **G**oal. Even, the donor nations are no more giving out loans and financial aids.

Unfortunately, academic institutions are churning out incompetent graduates (professionally) every year into the already oversaturated labour market. It would have been a different story if these crops of fresh graduates are taught practical/practicable entrepreneurial development courses at the last year of their sojourn at schools. On arriving to the labour market after service, **most dream of non-existing white and blue collar jobs.** After **fruitless search for jobs**, they give up to idleness. **Frustration leads many into crimes** (economic/financial, social, political, technological, spiritual crimes). Ironically, they are endowed with one talent or the other. Advisably, they can develop this from small to medium to big business. That is the ladder those reigning big businesses climbed to get there. Most of them (the victims of bad leaders-the employable unemployed) are aware of this but they have **the fear of start-up capital** and poor, ineffective and inefficient social infrastructure. The fear of starting a **one-man business** in a piecemeal/small and develop abide with him/her. Therefore, they remain idle and roam the streets for unavailable **jobs**. **Devil, they say, finds job for idle minds and idle hands.** Some have **beautiful ideas** to develop into businesses, but the **dearth of capital** remains **the bane.** Unfortunately, governments abandon their priorities to provide working infrastructure at a cheap cost for the masses for planning to employ a few hands into the government Ministries, Departments and Agencies instead of creating employment opportunities for the fresh graduates and skilled citizens.

In retrospect, **this book is proffering the needed solutions** to these sets of people, every reader of this socio-economic—researched based book will find it a scripture that they cannot afford to part with.

Teasers

The search for **jobs** to sustain herself led **Roselyn, 29,** a **single parent** of one, a **Food Technologist graduate** from a university, to work at a eatery, after three months of probation, she was relieved of the **job** pending the time the dwindling income of the firm start to go back to normal to enhance paying the new staff. **Roselyn** was back on the street disappointed even though she has already been **ostracised by age limit** to get government and many other private companies' **jobs** as replacement. There is no thank to badly implement economic policies, sit-tight syndrome among some leaders particularly in **Africa** and the poor state of the infrastructure in some and absence from many nations especially in the third world nations. **Roselyn** only needs to think and do like **Mr. John Stith Pemberton** with her professional skills to be self-employed!

Generally speaking, hardly can one see a nation that does not have the problem of unemployment. Though, most of these nations have natural **jobs** to develop. For instance, many drought threatening nations in **Africa** have **history** to tell the world about their **civilization and cultural heritage.** This is a **tourist attraction** that can fetch such hard currencies. Many have **undeveloped and untapped human**

intellects that could have made them **Japan of Africa!** A talent discoverable or a skill known with them is hot cake in many wealthy nations across the globe; ironically, unemployment is a national problem threatening the existence of their nation. Truthfully, in these nations, enhancing infrastructures are grossly inadequate even in the advanced economies; the infrastructures have been overstretched due to more immigrants under different asylums visas. To this writer, it is unfortunate and seems absurd that graduates and the skilled men still complain about the scourge when it is not necessary. Imagine what a graduate and talented person would become if such can set up and apply what he/she has learnt from schools in the course of establishing the **job.** Today we have graduates who are gifted in knitting that have established knitting and embroidery business developing from a small scale to a large scale. They started from knitting for retailers in schools and public places to become big firm. The first capital is got from the clients to buy all materials (needle, thread and wools) needed. Many graduates fail to turn their profession into a skill and reality! This is unlike the likes of **Zukerbergs** and other tech-entrepreneurs. Those who think same are not lucky as **Mark Zukerberg** and his friends who co-founded **Facebook** as their own government never provided the working social infrastructures to be creative! The advanced nations are concentrating more in the building of effective infrastructure that could enhance provision of **new jobs** for the idlers especially **the youths** who are **social risks** to all administrations and the nation! The underdeveloped nations blessed with corrupt administrators are busy looting the treasury and selling public property to themselves and their cronies! To save the nations from the adverse effects of the scourge of unemployment, we deemed it fit to open the eyes of those who thought that no business out there can be done without capital. We have done our invaluable socio-economic research which shows that there are businesses that the idlers can start doing without a dime! Remember again, **Warren Buffett and many American billionaires started without a dime but ideas! The taste of the pudding is in the eating'**, the maxim says. **Happy reading!!**

FREQUENTLY ASKED QUESTIONS

Q. How is it possible to start any business without a dime?

A. Does a nomad need a dime to start rearing cattle which are gifts (from people to him) at his birth or as inheritance from his parents? Does a child of a farmer need capital to get freehold lands and local farm tools in their village to have a large plantation? What about the children of fishermen? . . . Do these set of guys need any capital to start their **inherited/communal jobs?** *Not at all! Therefore many innate* **jobs** *do not need a dime to start except those who are covetous to have white and blue collar* **jobs!** *Meanwhile, for the latter, he must have a source of earning a stipend to eat little even once, at least in a day, either from a parent, close relation, rich or average individual, spouse, friend, colleague, neighbour . . . or a responsible government or spiritual leader even if one is a refugee!* **Every man likes to be independent** *to maintain his reputation hence the mind of one who* **desires to be his own boss** *especially if such has a hobby, skill, talent . . .to develop into a* **job!** *Such must sacrifice part of his earnings per day for a target number of days or weeks to earn enough that can buy some tools needed. For instance, a writer needs to save* **about five hundred and sixty Nigeria Naira (Four American Dollars)** *in a month to buy a writing pad, a biro, a compact disk/flash drive and pay cost of typesetting to collate a story or more (Just a sacrifice of twenty Naira per day). This is just a* **nest egg!** **All works (tangible items/ services) start from reducing ideas into black and white (writing)!** *Enter your work into prized* **contests** *within or outside, if you win in one, such money is enough to start publishing business of your other stories. Secondly, all growing* business needs a **broker/agent**. *Get one who believes in your work to get you a sponsor for an agreement. Sincerely yours, this writer got his work written, search for publishers abroad, got the one with the best royalty package, and secured the partner in a broker who got a sponsor. The agreement was written on how to share the royalties. This was how it all started! Bear it in mind,* **all jobs from talents, skills, ability, ideas . . . need an agent to get a financier!** *Agents need continual social networking to succeed. Read on and see how another talented writer made big sum of money from entering a contest what he wrote with empty (hungry) stomach!* **Enter into contests** *with your typed works and that could be a good avenue to start-up. We call the agent/broker as* **agent for social resources** *to meet. Lastly, you can* **sell patient right** *of one of your works to start and develop the rest just as* **Kiichiro Toyota, Sakichi's son,** *did to get started (read about him in the last page). Summon courage to start small just as renowned business moguls of this planet.* **Brian Tracy** *wrote* **"To be a big business success, you must first be a small business success. To sell many items at high prices, you must first sell a few items at low prices".** *To be a man is not a day* **job** *beside* **Rome** *is not built in a day!*

Q. Assuming the person has other talents other than writing and researching which demand for more money to get the tools, what would such do?

A. Firstly, work on the choicest talent. Every investment needs personal sacrifice (prudency) of the owner. We simply mean **'moral and financial discipline'**. Such should involve himself in some casual/helping/broker **jobs** (in this book) to get some capital to start. In other way, let him take a longer time to save (from his sustenance allowance) what he needed to start from his little earning to feed per day. Remember that no matter how bad the economy is, you must have a basic allowance from parents, guardians, friends, government or an individual. With a little savings from that, you should be able to **raise an amount** (nest egg) to get your work **reduced into black and white!** Little consistent **drops of water make an ocean**, the saying goes. Obey **George Classon's** admonition in his popular book **"The Richest Man in Babylon"**. **Pay yourself 10% as a monthly salary and invest the rest 90%** when you start making revenue no matter how little. Aside this, there are numerous useful materials around you that are rotten away. Strive to work on converting those wasting wastes to wealth through **selling** some or **rent/lease** it out to get some required funds to get the relevant tools. Meanwhile, ensure you invest to acquire more skills/knowledge on your choice of **job.** The greater the knowledge, the greater the skills, the more the monetary value for the skills. Therefore, invest to have more knowledge at the initial stage. **Re-invest, reinvest and re-invest, then start saving for future from acquiring disposable assets.** That is the bird that lays the golden egg. After getting more income, channel the bulk to the expansion of that **job** as it is a great mistake investing such in another person's **job.** Read another title from the same author titled **'waste to wealth jobs'** to have the details with relevant practical illustrations as it is outside the scope of this work! You could otherwise **'sell'** skills or **one of your ideas** to get started even **the patent rights** on condition! Borrow a leaf from a person like **Kiichiro Toyota** who sold patent rights to start **Toyota incorporation.** In ancient rural **Nigeria**, fathers engaged some of his sons to farm in order to sponsor the younger ones to school. Were you in their shoes, is that not worth doing? It is a rural attitude for elderly ones to cultivate large expanse of lands and sell the produce to sponsor the younger ones to schools. Some responsible elders do so at the absence/demise of their father. A family can spend all the income to **finance a talent or skill**. **The talent could feed them for generation!** Husband can set up a business for the family based on an identified innate or acquired/professional skill. An identified talent in a family can become the source of wealth if nurtured. A mentor, **El Mubassir Abdulsalam,** a Quantity Surveyor by profession, but highly talented in writing, at the time he was in dire need of **job** (unemployed), wrote six short stories to positively spend his time, typeset the work from the little saved from his daily expenses on the basics, submitted the story in a national short story contest and eventually won the best **Association of Nigerian Authors (2002)** short story of the year with a cash prize of **One Hundred Thousand Naira!** This is more than enough to start self-publishing! I started my first publication with crowd funding (tokens from three friends) and the next with just **fifteen thousand naira (Equivalent of 96 US dollars)** realized from selling a four-page children story! Alternatively, if you cannot <u>sell a story</u> or <u>enter</u> your work in <u>prized contests</u> to win big money to start up, then **seminars** can be **organised for a fee** to raise enough money (capital) to start up/expand the most desirous business. Another method is through packaging a very **attractive proposal** to interested individuals, corporate organisations or political bigwigs on your choice project as that could be the attraction to the would-be investor! You are advised to read text to write persuasive proposals.**" Good proposals are expensive and time consuming"** according to **Tom Sant**, the author of **Persuasive Business Proposals** (2004, 85-87: second edition) Above all, set a target (with time) of what you are going to become in term of wealth hence you have a financial and reputation worth! **If you cannot negotiate your skills/talents worth, employ an agent.** Many **professional skills** are enough to generate revenue to start big on the **job** later. Imagine what a stenographer, typesetter (very quick in typesetting) copy editor . . . can make if they can turn round their professional skills by **'selling'** them (**mobile service**) out to raise fund to start/ expand theirs as employers. You can even sell an asset, given as gift, self-acquired or inherited to take off. **Peter Drucker** was reported to have said: *"When you see a successful business, someone once took a big risk"*

Q. When you emphasize that friends and families are the first set of clients for a new business owner, what about a situation where such is a refugee in a town/nation that he does not understand the terrain (language)?

A. Yes, friends and families first. A business owner in a refugee camp has friends among the inmates and those attending to them. A refugee, even an asylum seeker, political or economic in a country, needs to produce what those people (aborigines) are interested in and he has spoken the language they understand (the products or service). His good product will surely draw their attention to him and hence get patronage. Such should however apply the **three T's (Truthful, Transparent and Trustworthy)** *as good moral precept is enough to endear one to people. These help a lot to have good credit rating to get free money towards building a nest egg.*

Q. Where does a collector of items so desired get market (buyers)?

A. We are in a global village. A little save from your stipend (nest egg) would expose your items to the buyers worldwide via the internet services (browsing, surfing, bulk short message service (SMS), social networks like **facebook, twitter . . .** It never costs a bulk of money in any denomination to pay for few hours searching for buyers! What you lack in term of capital, someone next door has it idle in bank accounts. I tell you he is looking for a dreamer like you whose work he desires to invest in as partner. The reason is simple; **he does not like his money stagnant. He is looking for somebody to increase the value of his wealth instead of keeping it idle in banks!**

Q. How can I make enough money you call living wage when you want me to be contented with peanuts at the beginning?

A. As the saying goes **'if you want to reach the highest, you have to start from the lowest.'** *Sincerely yours, many successful people today started like that but I would like the involvement of the government of each nation to pass a bill on the minimum amount to be paid for a talent and a self-employed person. With this in place, people would surely be adequately remunerated and that alone serves as a great motivation. In short, be contented with small price initially, those who paid you stipends in the beginning will later pay you in hard currencies when you become a star! Alas, you have **a story** of encouragement **to tell** the next generation of entrepreneurs as you would have become a role model in business! Again since our focus is **zero-capital job**, remember that some skills/products demand* paying **partly in advance**, *this is how clients finance **jobs**/businesses. Become a celebrated writer like the* **Soyinkas, Achebes** *and you get **paid in advance** for your work. They build the reputation gradually, start building yours too! Another way to get paid for a **job** well done is to organize a **free** seminar, acting a play for free at chosen location for selected rich people for leisure. Many worship places are doing this to make money. They secure a good hall. Advertise and package events that they believe will attract a target audience considering their status, career and financial buoyancy. After a good show, people voluntarily pay for the show! If you are drafted to a show by organizer for free, let the compere/ master* *of ceremony with the organizer be aware, tell them to solicit money from the audience after the wonderful act and you will see the gains in monetary term after the show! Think how you can attract the minds of your viewers or listeners to make money from them. They will spray mints on you!* **Free shows/exhibitions** *pay sometimes more than a ticketing show! Lastly, you can take over a dying business with a persuasive/convincing proposal to the original owner that the business needs expertise knowledge and management of yours to outlive the owner(s) aside the incomes that will not cease to come.* **Try one.**

Q. Again, in a situation where one does not have any client at all, how can one build client base for one's service?

A. Start from man–client service. With your technically sound skill, be polite and courageous to approach him. He will give you a trial; your performance on the **job** as you deliver quality would surely endear you to him. He 'sells' your good service to others. Within a couple of weeks, your clients would increase. Your satisfactory services and products speak volume about you. Again, a satisfied client would surely broadcast your service. Just as scriptural **Joseph** was mentioned before Pharaoh by an inmate (publicist)you have your clients increase in number, they would recommend your work (products or services) to **K**ings, **P**residents, **C**EOs . . . They are your unpaid/non–commissioned **P**ublic **R**elation **O**fficers. Visit big corporation and make a request about their first sales and customers, you will get to know that they started to rise gradually. **A male child grows to become a father. He never walks and talks on his first day on the planet-earth!** Sometimes, do not give outrageous bill as your clients could, most probably, satisfied clients pay more than you ever thought based on the quality and finesse! Tell them to pay your worth, then, **you will get to know that your worth is invaluable!**

Q. What is your major reason for clamouring for self-employment?

A. *That is best form of employment that can solve the scourge of unemployment, a top priority of the* **M***illennium* **D***evelopment* **G***oals.* **It is a self-challenge.** *The greatest joy is* **self-worth** *as you are not under anybody's control and* management. *In other word, you are a boss and would soon* **become boss** *and mentor/role model for others when you expand. Imagine the status and the accolades that trail the office of the* **P***resident/***C***hairman/***C***hief* **E***xecutive* **O***fficer! You determine the nature of your* **job**, **job** *schedules,* **job** *ethics and policies, the target income, time to open and time to retire.* **What one under an employer (salaried worker) makes in twenty years can be made with ease by you in ten years! Dream it, realize it!**

N.B. Readers should collate all the eight major ways to start up in the FAQs just read before proceeding.

> 'Self-employment worths doing
> But talents and skills matter a lot
> Selling and marketing them is it
> To get started with zero dime
> To be free from the dictates
> The dictates of capitalists
> The determiners of what you produce and sell
> And even the quality, quantity and the price!'

WHAT IS A JOB?

Knowledge has no limitation. This could be the reason why **the noblest that had walked the crust** admonished mankind that **'knowledge seeking is from cradle to grave',** womb to tomb precisely. **'It is a must for both male and female'** so he sermoned. What an ethnic calls **'fini'** meaning **'end'**, another calls it **'fini'**, another calls it **'fin'** whereas the last means another thing (tail) to an English man! **Different windows open to the world** so that different folks would have different tales. Our perception of a thing always differs especially in the definition of the word **'JOB'**. Different scholars from different discipline, especially the social scientists, propounded and defined **JOB** according to their <u>academic backgrounds, nations or climes, time, event, ethnical cultural values or tradition, belief and many other factors</u>. Some ethnics in northern **Nigeria** see farming and hunting as pastime **JOBS** to their real profession of teaching, trading . . . Some take to bee-keeping, some get fun from keeping domestic/ornamental pets as pastime, some even tame wild animals without considering turning such into a paying **JOB**. Some like green environment and so plant ornamental and medicinal trees and flowers of different aroma yet never give it a trial to turn this hobby or turn-on interest into **JOBS.** Many are naturally good in settling disputes and counselling people, an activity that can pay their bills, yet they take them as pastimes. One good thing about them is that they derive **joy and enthusiasm** from the activities. Unfortunately, these are among the numerous who are still looking for **JOBS** that are in **'SHORT SUPPLY** or unavailable' in many cases to accommodate all the unemployed at a go. In short, most of them have other things they call **JOBS!** Those riverside-living ethnics see fishing, cash crops plantation, lumbering and canoe building as their natural **JOBS, swimming** is a pastime. This is unlike the same swimming that makes good names and money for the **Australian Michael Phelps** of the modern world. Total housewives especially those in purdah do not work outside at all to make a living, the husbands work to sustain the family while those women at home are satisfied with the **JOB** at home which including nurturing the children (since **child—raising is proved to be bigger challenge than child—bearing)**, their **JOBS** are at home-front which they do with satisfaction. Had they found wanting in carrying out their duties (**jobs** at home), the families will suffer and that would have negative effects on the society. Family is the basis unit of a society. **When a family gets domestic problem, it reflects in the society. When home is corrupt, it tells on the society!** Back on the inevitable roles and potentials of housewives at homes, many a good cook among housewife would be employer of labour and spread the professional skills if they desire to start like the **Atlanta Georgia** born Pharmacist **John Stith Pemberton**, the founder of **COCACOLA INCORPORATION** and many professionals including chefs today. He started from 'home' most probably his 'kitchen'.(Read extensively from another title from the same author **'Housewives are potential entrepreneurs'**) Husband and wife develop **Tantalizer**, another couple established **Tastee Fried Chickens,** and these are fast food/eateries or **Q**uick **S**ervice **R**estaurants in **Nigeria**. We have seen two blood sisters who co-founded fashion house. Like **the Toyotas** in **Japan**, **the Majins** (mother and her two daughters) in **Nigeria** developed their interests. To them, **'fashion is passion'**. Every **T**om, **D**ick and **H**arry is aware of music generation in **Fela Anikulapo Kuti's** family. Today, many music and entertainment stars in **N**igeria, living or deceased have their children taking the batons. **Dan Maraya in Jos in Nigeria** is a one-man band. We have seen one man shows in comedians. Abound are many dramatic monologues. Many aged relax at evenings under shed playing local games as a pastime what today's sportsmen are making money and fame as a sporting business. Imagine **Michael Phelps**, the **great swimmer** from **Australia**; imagine the **endorsements** and the **wealth** of **Tiger Woods** from golf and **David Beckhams** from football! Many stories are told as folklores for fun which is a source of income for people today. Some are naturally funny and could outwit world renowned **Bill Cosby, Benny Hilly** . . . but do that as pastime and not a profession. <u>The only turn off to the audience is a shaggy-dog story.</u> Comedians should avoid that to win the hearts of spectators. In short, whatever one derives joy and satisfaction from while doing it like the charity-based organisations, whatever you do and get desired satisfaction, maybe profits, from is a **JOB.** Your **skill/ talent** is **a capital asset,** put passion and time to develop it into a lucrative **job!**

A JOB is therefore a specialisation or a profession, a calling or vocation and all that one involves in at a particular time that provides the doer satisfaction, joy, passion and earnings enough to offset his bills and make some savings. What you make a living, by giving efforts and knowledge, from is also regarded as a **JOB**. What you have passion for is a **JOB. Emerson** was reported to have said: *"Nothing great was ever accomplished without enthusiasm".* Religious leaders are doing reformation **jobs.** Domestic servants help a don to attain his set goal at the set time therefore are doing **jobs.** The coach and technical crew on the bench at the stadium are great mathematicians on seat. The audience applauding the athletes with passion are thrilling them to perform hence doing hectic **job** without a pay! Likewise the activities of many charity-centred non-governmental organisations across the globe, they have passion for what they are known for and that is the joy of doing the charitable work **(job)!** Generally, **job** could be profit centred even many **N**on-**G**overnmental **O**rganizations, mobile or static **jobs**, leisure or idle-enhanced **jobs** (mostly negative), male—dominated/centred or female—centred **jobs,** faith—based or secular **jobs,** nationalized or internationalized **jobs**, voluntary or involuntary **jobs,** vocational or technical **jobs** aside the categories you are going learn of later in the book.

For limitation of purpose, in the light of this work, *a JOB is an activity that earns the doer a living wage. A living wage is an amount that offsets the bills of the working person.* The bills include all the three basic needs (food, shelter, clothes) then which today include Medicare, transportation and communication expenses. If such earning cannot provide those needs, then such is not categorised as a **JOB** even for those living with disabilities. Disables are only physically challenged; they can become entrepreneurs or employees for others.

Meanwhile, a **living wage** varies from one clime to another just as definition of **jobs** and business' categorisation. In this piece, we are not referring charity-based business as a **job.** We are rolling out **jobs** that can fetch **living wage** to the doers if well packaged, marketed and distributed to the right users as they want them at the right time! But, they should learn the trick of starting small and be **prudent** in spending.

> 'Use your limbs
> Apply your thinking faculty
> Including your other senses/intelligence quotient
> Develop an interest that tallies with others (target clients)
> Profit or charity centred
> And you've started a job!'

WHO DOES A JOB?

Candidly speaking, **everyone does a job, positive or negative, fulltime or part time, able or disable!** This is clear from the general category listed above. All youths in the streets are engaged in one form of **'job'** or the other. Some are impacting positively to the nation while some negatively! Those with certificates, regardless of courses of study, and those that have no qualifications; Those with natural skills and those that acquired professional skills; Those living in the urban and those in the village; The children of the rich and those of the poor; all partake in an activity or the other, profit based or mere charity! In our own language of this work, a person, with natural innate and acquired skills, techniques, certificates from academic institutions (vocational, technical . . .) and such could either be physically fit or not, does a **job.** It is favourably disputed that disability is not inability. Every man has one potential or the other that needs to be discovered, by oneself, people or an institution, and nurtured. Emphasizing the latter, a blind can be trained to read and write; use his limbs to do vocational **jobs** to earn legitimate money, same to a cripple who can use his **five senses** to lay his hands on a lucrative business. Wealthy and famous, charismatic **John Foppe,** the world renowned motivational speaker is armless! We have seen many singers of repute that are blind. Remember the internationally renowned singer, **Steve Wonder** in **France** and our own **Dan Maraya in Jos, Nigeria!** Many stars are churning out every now and then from **Paralympics** and games for the physically-challenged people. What efforts are put in place to test what stays in their upstairs. Unfortunately, most end up begging for alms along the streets! Social nuisance, I call them. Wasting inestimable human resources before our own eyes! Application of the senses and the efforts of the limbs bring legitimate earnings, period!

Summarily, **jobs** are for all even the aged regardless of the physical strength. **Wages and salaries** could be different for many reasons according to the economists. In a developing nation like Nigeria, a worker who is earning **over fifty thousand naira** monthly could not be able to meet his financial obligation because of the rising inflation rate in the economic system that devalues the currency unlike another worker in the **United States** that is earning **two thousand dollars** with favourable economic system. If the former cannot meet his **basic needs,** transportation, communication and with some savings for the rainy day, then such does not have a **job.** In the latter, if **two thousand dollar** is enough to meet all the needs of the worker including savings for a rainy day, then, he surely has a lucrative **job!**

There is a tendency that such person whose monthly earnings cannot meet his needs to be tempted to become fraudulent like diverting the official time for his personal use, using official equipment under him for his own unofficial use aside the temptation to embezzle or misappropriate the public funds! For a worker earning little to get more without illicit means, such has to **overwork** his limbs and brains. The anger within the angry man's mindset could result into social unrest. **Overworking,** according to the legislation of **International Labour Organisation (ILO),** beyond eight hours have adverse effects on the health of such person. The result is retirement earlier than expected hence the reduction in the **Gross Domestic Product.** The wealth distribution would not be able to go round the people and the nation suffers the heat in security risks. In addition, such who is earning very big sum of remuneration but could not get satisfaction and shows **no passion for the job** is still unemployed. Such is yet to be employed!

> 'I fear the nation, this nation of course!
> Whose youths' time not occupied
> Positively to do positive things
> Else they spent priceless time doing negative
> At the peril of the nation's next generation!'

1.3 KINDS OF JOBS AT A GLANCE

Based on our socio-economic research findings analysis, we categorise the **jobs** for people into these:

(a) Needs-induced jobs

Do you care to identify the needs/wants of people around you? Do you listen to their complaints (problems)? Do you empathise with such needs/problems? Do you make the best use of what you overheard at newspaper vendor stands to kick start a business idea? Do you mix with your age group freely without listening to their urgent needs? From those responses for the questions, you should be able to start doing a thing and leave the midst of idlers. Those needs would surely create avenues for your own building a business empire from the scratch. Take these few samples: you hear people complaint on dullness of environment, don't you foresee that they need some entertainers like amusing comedians, entertaining sportsmen, singer . . . that can spice up their lives and replace the dull moment into a charged one. Imagine some complaints on filths in the park, charitable work in this case could fetch you regular income if you meet the appropriate authority to give you the endorsement for a fee to keep it clean and tidy. Same to gridlock on the busy road, turn yourself into a volunteer traffic worker and before you know it some cents, shilling or kobo could fill your pocket! Some motorists could help you secure a **job** in that line. Just take it, needs are solvable problems which create **job** opportunities. The more the needs/problems, which are unlimited unless creatures cease to exist, the more the **jobs** opportunities. Look out for needs to start thinking about the solutions. Do it with passion. Needs are what your target clients are having deep, inevitable interest in. Sincerely yours, the need to expose idle youths to numerous **jobs** they can do even without capital prompt me to start researching on those categories of **jobs**. This is one of the products. I know that the major obstacle to set up business here where government and financial institutions are not up to task towards provision of capital made me work on different **jobs** that can be set up with zero-capital!

(b) **Policy/budget-induced jobs**

Policy statements by a government and executive official could make the unemployed ones get **jobs** or open ways to start or develop new **jobs**. Policies are on all facets of life. On health, environment, education, security and all other issues political, economic and social. In **Nigeria**, the common statement of government at all levels is direct to the graduates to be self-employed. Government made it clear that it is incapable to provide **jobs** for the employable unemployed. I believe this policy is the same across the globe. Truly speaking, government supposes to create enabling atmosphere for people to thrive in their businesses. People can create **new jobs** from the existing ones provided they can create something unique to the existing business. We have seen a lady musician with pot in **Nigeria** aside the talking drummer lady, **ASA**. A sample is in a seller of a fried bean-cake mixed with egg (egg-flavoured bean-cake) in a street where bean-cake is fried with either groundnut oil or other s. If government is intended to have modern markets in their policy, **new jobs** would spread to those areas. If government decides to prolong provision of infrastructure to a place, every investor on infrastructure at the time would reap heavily from the delay. In a nation that electricity is not supplied or in short supply, like a population of over 150 million sharing less than five thousand megawatt in this twenty first century, sellers and the **agents/sales distributors** of alternatives (inverters, solar energy materials, wind energy and their bulbs) would make huge sales. **Sales agents** invest no dime to distribute to users at a profitable price if he understands how to play the game! Remember if you lack the technical knowledge and the tools, start from being **an agent** between seller/producers and users. Just watch the lips of those executives, in public or private, and you should be able to start a **job**. The lapses of an administration come out of their mouths or spokesmen especially their non-challant attitude to public service. I have explained this under the headline '**WHISPER?**' in the second volume. Every government and organization by their policies including their weak points creates direct and indirect **jobs**. It takes a wise that can analyse words that can learn to understand the **jobs** opportunities. Simply put, the system and direction of priorities of an administration create avenues to start a **job(s)**. Read the details about this in another title titled "**Wastes to wealth jobs**" by the same author. You will learn how to **read news, reports, columns, classified adverts, editorials and viewpoints** inside newspapers to fish out **jobs!**

(c) **Situation-enhanced jobs**

By this we mean events-enhanced **job** opportunities. Sometimes, it is done on contracts. Sometimes, it is done gratis. Sometimes, a **full-time job** and some other times, a **part-time job!** In a place where e xhibitions,seminars,symposia,conferences,meetings,worships,preac hings,crusades . . . that could pull crowd, especially tourist centres, sellers of basic needs especially food, drinks, stationery materials, gift items, souvenirs . . . would sell, hence a ground of creating good **jobs** for producers and sellers/distributors. What about sad events, especially natural disasters, political impasse in a nation . . ., these need to be reported or documented to create **jobs**. Many idle youths in the world need to have explored the slippery opportunities to be engaged in a positive thing (Read more in our title: '**Wastes to wealth jobs**' by the same author) A glaring sample is manufacturers who are having sleepless nights for not making enough sales. Can you create brokerage **job** out of this situation? Think of all situations that could ignite the flame of engaging yourself positively.

(d) **Technology-driven jobs**

The greater advancement the technology, the greater the number of innovation and their products for the use of people to improve their standard of living. The more the extent of innovation, the more the number of technicians/repairers for different electronics. Just imagine the number of **jobs** being created daily in **China** and the other **Asian Tigers**. Herbal and water technology are providing employment opportunities for millions on the crust today! Generally, all continents of the world are endowed with technological resources. The ability to transform such into good use differs. This alone makes the **western world** the **hub** of technological development even though the **Asians** are fastly catching up with them! With the level of technology in **Western Europe** and **America,** it is hard to hear that millions are still unemployed when they could create **jobs** from the existing **jobs** in millions! This writer can! Innovations in technology is creating bigger avenue to start new **jobs** for the youths roaming the streets wasting irreversible and priceless time resource. Many developing technological giants started from dismantling and re-coupling of a technological output. I read about **Chrysler Chevrolet** how he started. **Sakici Toyota** improved on the product of European automatic loom to start his. What stops many technical graduates from working on a tool or gadget, dismantle it and think on improving it. Let him reduce that into writing first before he employs any of the eight ways already taught in the **FAQs** to start a business without his personal capital! In most cases, apply the **OPMs** (taught later in the book) to start. Read for more exposition in one of his titles titled '**New jobs from the existing jobs**'

(e) **Innate-enhanced jobs**

This is one of the kinds of **JOBS** one can start without a dime that are exposed to readers in this volume. They provide more **jobs** and the foundation of all existing **jobs**. A nation with naturally gifted people should create millions of **jobs** rather than having dearth of unemployment. There are **jobs** that many idlers in the streets can start instead of searching for non-existing **jobs** in the labour market. We shall endeavour to collate the steps to take by a state of about five millions people to generate over one million new **jobs** in a year in one of our subsequent publications by God's infinite grace. These **jobs** do not require certificates but the application of the **five senses** with the contribution of the limbs. Today, from **Africa,** some renowned traditional gods' priests are lecturers in university abroad. Many a linguist is due on the payroll of many international organisations whereas they never attend a convectional school in their native country. Numerous are musicians, lyricists and many artistes that have become part-time lecturers. Whatever you do, create a niche for yourself. If plaiting of hairs run in the veins of your family, open a hair plaiting salon. It is hightime we had such salon as auto salon, wood salon, nail salon . . . . This is specialization that could give you an edge! Make a household name for your field! Some are used in films just for the costumes and dialects being spoken that are fortunately part of the script written by the writer. I embarked on writing and self-publishing this piece after a few years of research when a government agency in charge almost frustrated my efforts to get it done through it.

In short, your **talents** provide you **jobs** than your acquired certificates. Your certificates would surely give you a lift and renders great help in nurturing the **innate talents** to reality. Some develop hobbies from their talents without the awareness. Today, we have seen medical doctors by training that have abandoned their stethoscopes for pen as they derive their satisfaction (fulfillment, joy and passion) from writing for readers of literatures; prized columns for print media and scripts on research—based issues. Give devil his due, they are more popular and widely accepted and patronised from what they write, publish and delivered.

To be candid, natural talents (technical or vocational skills/abilities, gifts, intellects) and collections of items often regarded as wastes have the capacity to provide **jobs** for millions and hence feed millions directly and indirectly. It takes a few geniuses in the advanced and the advancing nations in the world to create lucrative **jobs** for their people! For instance, a creative writer of good story/research writer is an asset to provide **jobs** those in on-line publishing, on-line marketing, on-line distribution, on-line advertising, transport, information and communication technology aside those who desire to have such material in documentary and movie! Many e-libraries have been established to create **jobs** for workers therein. This has helped many tutors to have e-lectures and e-training. What does it take a nomad to start rearing cattle he inherited from his father? How much will it cost a child of farmers to start farming in their villages? Of course, not a dime except little persuasion! It is poke-nosing into the lives in the city since there are no inducements on the part of the government to provide working social infrastructures and good prices for their products that are chasing them away from the natural inherited **jobs** to start looking for **white collar jobs** that are in short supply in the city! **Tourism** is a good source of injection of foreign wealth into the local economy provided the sector's potentials are discovered and well nurtured (packaged, branded, advertised) to attract tourists and researchers/students from all over the world! Private investors could be persuaded with good policies to invest in the sector to create employment opportunities.

(f) **Clime/environ—induced jobs**

A man living in an area with wide mass of fertile, sea for irrigation abundant rainfall and moderate climatic condition need not be faulted if he chose to be a large scale farmer. Imagine another where you have grassland and brooks, no blame if such is a shepherd. His clime determines the type of **job** a man should engage in. A young lad from a rural that changes his environ to a family of elite in the urban would have interest to go to school or at worst learn the language of communication in the new environ. The earlier he conforms, the better for him in life. Manufacturing sites or the industrial areas are a good base for artisans like labourers, rewires, bricklayers, carpenters, electricians, technicians, food sellers, hawkers . . . especially those who can collect technical information for publication of some publishers of journals. Many tourists' and miners' attraction sites abound in villages that can be turned to money-making ventures and for provision of **job** opportunities for the unemployed. Events like mountain climbing, dance drama events, exhibition of cultural activities, delicacies, entertainment, arts and science (technology) to the worlds. Let each village head/ government of such district sponsors this in partnership with business minded organization to create seasonal but lucrative **jobs** and discover talents/skills. Many a traditional sports can be launched to the acceptance of tourists. Tourists' attraction will open up such village/town for economic purpose and gains (success). People living in the cold region need raincoats, cardigans and the stuff. Imagine the amount the weaver of such could reap from supplying these people in need. People migrate to **Europe** for green pasture as they believe they will get **jobs** even if they are **'dirty' jobs** in advanced economies than staying put in their respective undeveloped poor nations. By the word **'dirty'**, we mean **social jobs** that should be for those who have very lower certificates, for instance, a trained accountant doing cleaning **job** but if he enjoys doing it with great interest and passion and the earning is paying his bills and could make some savings for a rainy day, he has found his **natural job**. Even though in general view, such **job** is below his standard and status in all measure but at least to attack poverty for one who does not have interest at all. It is a dirty **job** yet **'a loaf of bread is better than a pebble of stone'**, a maxim says. In short, as man migrates, tendency to engage in another activity that butters his bread is greater. Over **twenty three—millions** of the unemployed in **Europe** should think within same to millions in hundreds in **Africa, Australia** and **Asia.** Individuals could create **jobs** from the existing **jobs** aside the categorized **jobs** in this book!

(g) **Cultural/belief-enhanced jobs**

Cultures are as old as the age. Culture is a tradition of an ethnic group. What the people say (language), eat, do or act individually or in group. An axiom rightly says: **"One man's food is another man's poison.** Many cultures across the globe are so rich that from the dialects exist **jobs** and path to create **jobs**. One can easily study their needs, strength and weak points for **jobs** to be created. This writer had heard of a man who served in a **'land of snails'** which was a town where it was a taboo to eat snails. Unfortunately, snails bred in thousands there. The wise man just abandoned his certificate for marketing of the snails to hotels in the urban towns' hotels, hostels and for individuals. He got the buyers, induced the children of the village to collect the snails, packed into sacks and with his transport allowance transported the packs to the urban where he did the selling. He made fortunes from the business.

(h) **Historical-induced jobs**

This is summarily **hereditary jobs.** This is passed from ethnic to ethnic, family to family, nation to nation, as this will give room to specialisations hence comparative cost advantages. Many are born into mining precious stones for many generations. Does such need to do another **job?** Some generation of miners identify the 'tribes' and 'classes' of the stones and their uses just as parents identify their identical twins! Those were farmers passed the methods of farming to the next generation. Certain nations today are identified with certain crop. **Gambia** is known with **groundnut. Cocoa and coffee** are to **Cote D'Ivoire.** Some towns in **Nigeria** are seen as the food baskets of the nation. **Kano** is centre of commerce. Had the new generation abandoned the path of their fathers and forefathers, where do we have the farmers to feed the populace today? What does a person whose fore-bearers are into a particular profession claiming that he is **jobless**? Numerous are **hereditary jobs** for people of the lineage. The drummers, artists, goldsmiths, blacksmiths, traditional songs singers for film makers, documentaries, events and personality (kings, warriors, priests, rich, . . .)We have seen graduates that have taken the **jobs** of their fathers and mothers when they could not secure lucrative **white and blue collar jobs!** There is no big deal in doing hereditary **jobs.** I doubt it if there is a family that is not endowed. The creator is so Beneficient that He endows all with one gift or the other. **No man/nation is left without a natural endowment.** Man only needs to learn to discover or his own or that of his family, lineage, town and nation to be engaged. Every family has a history in which embedded their natural activities that they suppose to do. Sometimes in the languages of all tribe exist what such ethnic should specialize on. Naturally, this is division of labour to have comparative cost advantage and goods and services flood the markets. **Nothing is created idle.** Have you heard of a village in the heart of vast farmland in **China's** eastern **ZHEJIANG PROVINCE** whose secret of making millions of dollars is in where deadly snakes like cobras, vipers and pythons are deliberately raised for food and medicine **(Reuters/**

The Punch, Thursday, June 23, 2011).There is purpose for all creatures in existence. Every man should work in synergy so also all kinds of **jobs** that will make life very easy and peaceful to live in. Many are innate meant to be discovered as the scope of this work. If a tradition/art is the most selling in your village/family, sell it after rebranding it!

> *"Cudgels the brains o'er the above*
> *Have you identified jobs awaiting the idlers?*
> *Suffice to fish out those ones intended*
> *Those with zero capitals*
> *Thinking how to start?*
> *Read on, oh dear reader!'*
> *Cry not for no job*
> *In the midst of plenty jobs, there are*
> *A little meditation on the above suffice*
> *Idle head and hands are devil's tool and room*
> *Hightime you got engaged"*

2.1. STARTING BUSINESS WITHOUT A DIME, IS IT FEASIBLE?

The answer is simply 'YES'! You just need some ideas and moral (integrity, kindness and the three P's). Remember that ideas rule the world. Those with great ideas make a great breakthrough. Get this clear first and get this at the back of your mind. No doubt, capital is the life-wire to direct the affairs of any business even the charity-centred ones. But, capital does not include the basic sustenance fees. To make money at the environment where capital cannot be assessed, then you need to work day and night to make some earnings first called **nest egg**. This is the reason why business that you can start without capital should be your first bet. Meanwhile, you must install this code in your brains-**TAGSORIs** where:

T stands for Talent. These are natural endowments on man and his environment. Just as man has talents so also the climes he lives. They are innate **ARTS**. That is what we referred to as the resources later in the code. We have been able to identify over thirty talents. These, among others, include writing, reading, speaking, running, walking, cooking, designing, painting, drawing, dancing, singing, chanting (poetry)acting, cooking, swimming and all sports activities, baking, preserving, teaching, imparting, sermoning, admonishing, listening, detecting, feeling, weaving(of hair, cloth, baskets, calabash, cane chair, broom . . .) mining, exploration, broadcasting, knitting, plaiting, collecting, decorating, narrating, interpreting (of dreams, events . . .), weightlifting, hunting, expedition, farming, comedy, cat walking, modelling . . . . With these, skills are created hence creativity.

N.B. A talent can feed the whole creatures! Just imagine the thousands that are feeding fat in writing from the table of the writer to the publishing firms and film/documentary/song producers, actors and actresses, costumiers, Information Communication Technology (ICT) people, financial houses, insurance and all stakeholders from the corporate responsibilities! . . .

Talents differ from man to man, place to place, ethnic to ethnic . . . The **Arabs** have crude oil and the intellectual property. **Japan** has human resources too not land resources as **Nigeria** that has both. **Africa** has good clime for farming hence industrialisation. Just maximise your talents and abilities. Develop talents that you have 'absolute comparative cost advantage' over others especially in the list of religion, entertainment and sports. Some centuries ago until the recent times, even though, technology is never a monopoly of any nation as all nations are endowed, yet, technology abounds more in **Europe**, particularly **Western Europe** simply because they provide favourable atmosphere to develop theirs! Today, many talents have given rise to skills worldwide particularly in **Asia!** How do we discover talents? This can be identified by oneself, one's parents or teachers or even a role model. It is discovered early in life or later. Where you have more than one talent, choose the one you always do as a hobby. That is where your interest lies! (Read this in another book of ours titled **'WASTES TO WEALTH JOBS'** by the same author)!

A stands for ability(physical strengths, inspiration, aspiration, dreaming . . .) and ability to gain new grounds, to be creative and versatile, to create large market share(advertising to win customers confidence and patronage),promotion,compete with rival competitors and to withstand the heat(adaptation),ability to apply the marketing mix(four P's) along with **the five R's(right—time, price, product, quantity, quality)** Ability to know your potentials (discover yourself for packaging and branding) and those you work or team up with, ability to study business the environ and time to start your business.You must have the ability to procure right raw materials, setting standard and target for yourself and business; ability to produce the right product at the right time and place for the right people (consumers); ability to re-write the history and creating a niche (Making a difference); ability to create new things (products, service, strategies . . .) to give consumers choices of products and services; ability to be prudence; doing periodical business assessment and development research and keeping of all records and data; ability to meet up the set standard by the regulatory authority; ability to manage people; ability to negotiate (bargaining) or employ an agent/broker to negotiate on your behalf and ability to identify and gain from your personal weak-points. In fact, the ability to bargain/negotiate could fetch you <u>brokerage **job** in your choice area of interest (sector)</u> within a shortest period of time! Weak-point, of yours or others, is a potential to start a **job.** Ability to listen to people and clients; ability to apply the senses at the appropriate time to identify the pressing needs (problems) of people and then proffer solutions would surely help/start to start a lucrative **job!** The sentence/statement **"I am capable!"** shows the ability. A trial leads into perfection and discovery. **"I am capable!"** means **"I am up to the task; I have the skills; I have the solutions; I will do it"**. That is the confidence to excel in a particular area of interest. Ability to traverse the earth helps a person to discover one self and new opportunities (break new grounds). It helps to get values to one's worth in term of resources. *What a nation has, another lacks. What a man is endowed with, another lacks!* In disability too, they say, is ability. This is natural to create synergy and social engineering and recognition! Lastly, ability to start small with ideas and practical experiences to start zero-capital business as taught in this work! Ability to reduce all the ideas that come to your head down for references and later development is a positive tool to start a **job**. The **Chinese** says *"The palest ink is stronger than the finest memory"* Ability includes aspiration, aspiration to be self-employed, self-made millionaire, aspiration to become employer of labours, aspiration to become a business/political guru . . . **Henry Ford** was quoted to have said: *"If you believe you can, or believe you cannot, in either case, you are probably right"*.

G stands for gifts (natural endowments) as lands and their resources, good climes which are referred to as free gifts of nature. Gifts include inherited wealth/cash from people, family, friends . . . . A good example is that of children of a nomad whose birthright gifts include herds of cattle, and lands, seeds to that of farmers. These are the social and economic resources around and within you!

S stands for skills, innate or the acquired/professional. The latter is those from the courses of studies by individuals. Innate skills are on being versatile and creative with the talents. Local swimmers like **Ijaw tribe in Nigeria** should train with other swimmers elsewhere to learn new tricks to excel. Mountain climbers in **Manbilla plateau in Nigeria** should practice with those climbing **Mountain Kilimanjaro**. Skills need being developed to world standard trend. Learn more learnable skills! To identify the skills, if your mind is positive that **'you can, then you can'**. With skills, let it be in your mind that 'You will'. You have the intelligence, intuition, innovation . . . to perform the task better than others! Your skill will give you the edge over others. Selling, reading, riding (cars, horse, bike . . .), cooking, tendering, preserving, hunting, fishing, expedition, speaking, writing, acting, singing and many other talents are skills. Many have talents but are not skillful as they left them unnurtured! Be wise like the **Toyota family of Japan. Sakichi's** invented automatic loom began the investment in **Toyota** vehicles, the highest selling automobile worldwide as at 2011. Most skill-enhanced profession does not require any capital to start. Such should start from doing **mobile service.** Then, let such be prudent as he/she set a target date to stop the service immediately he/she is able to raise enough capital to set up the business.

O stands for organising (major function in management) as in organising shows, seminars, symposia . . . . for target clients. A man with great talent needs to be well organised to catch the running train! Believe me, **you can organise seminars without spending a dime!** (Contact the author via e-mail)

R stands for resources, natural in human(social resource) as intellects, intuition, innovation, versatility, creativeness and other enviromental like favourable climes, fertile lands, peace, good policies . . . Land resources, aside the favourable climes, are the minerals within the crust, the medicinal and ornamental plants and animals including birds on the crust and in the air! The resource you must never fail to invest is your **TIME**. Time to discover yourself, your choice/preference, strength and weak points, time to mix with others to be aware of their needs as their needs would create avenue to start a **job!** Time should be devoted to get more training on your talent/skill or develop your idea, time to learn from others or consult with them. He who fails to invest his **irreversible TIME** resource has lost the inestimable resource that is costlier than all other resources! *A time lost is an opportunity lost forever!*

I stands for ideas, interest (hobbies), interest (in sharing feelings with your clients, work to solve their interest/problem) inquisition, intuitiveness, innovation, intelligence, investing all your resources wisely . . . . and lastly identify the need and problem of those in your/the environ to set up a business who are your target clients, invest not with your money but what **Brian Tracy** called "**sweat equity**". Ideas rule the world, they agreed upon. Idea is from the thought (in mind) which later becomes the tangible product or service. Whatever you see around is from an idea! The idea of **Kiichiro Toyota** to make money from selling patent right of his father's invention was the turning point in the history of **Toyota automobile! New ideas make a new business/job from the existing ones.**

N.B. If you do not have any talent or skill to develop, just pick up an interest in a thing or create an idea, then cudgel your brains on how to start positive **job** from such. Remember again that every single challenge/need paves way to start up an idea/business! Events around you could propel a business idea that would benefit the society and transform the nation! **Many successful inventors started from there!**

With just one or all of the above, you can start a **job** without investing a dime except your **EFFORTS, MORAL UPRIGHTNESS, PERSUASSION, CONVICTION** and **TIME**! Again, BEAR IT IN MIND, you must start small and start growing by each day.

A quarantined seed grows to become a multiple fruits as a tree—bearing fruit!

Get the maxim right, the **Chinese** says '**To remove the mountain, you start from picking the first stone'.** All business in mind start small, check their profiles. Ask **British** entrepreneur, **Richard Branson.** Consult the books of late **Steve Jobs** and many other great entrepreneurs. **Mark Zukerberg**, February 2004, started **facebook** from the dorm at **Harvard.** Today, after about seven years, he has about **eight hundred million** as **subscribers!** You should start from reducing that idea in you right now into writing first and be contented with that little for sustenance from your breadwinner. Sacrifice some token savings everyday from that stipend for future use to start that noble, unique idea being scripted. Do not refuse this admonition to script that idea in lines, it could vanish into thin and could never be recovered again! This is how this writer began and within a space of five years can boast of many achievements. You too can. Start from writing the reminiscence of your alma mater, what about life story of a good personality in sports, entertainment, religion; a school or institute; reporting voyages and adventures; observations from closeness to nature .... Sincerely yours, no writer can exhaust titles/issues to write about until the existence ceases! Develop an idea/issue to write about. Develop a solution to solve a need. That makes a good idea. **Cocacola** incorporation started from an idea of a man from his own home 'kitchen', by name **John Stith Pemberton.** He later served his invention for **five cents** per glass cup of soda wash at **Jacob's pharmacy!** Today, millions are earning fat salaries across the globe! Many are working and feeding fat from the remuneration from **Ford Company** in the world today whereas it (the automobile idea) got sourced from a mechanic workshop in country! Think of **Guinness, Peugeot, Mercedes, Toyota, Nissan, Mazda, Tata** . . . and all the variants of brands of all domestic goods and services across all sectors of the economy. Somebody started them. Later, co-founders. In most cases, they started when there were neither adequate social infrastructures nor incentive for firms to operate compare to what we have today as far as economic policies are concerned. Yet, they started small and are growing bigger year in year out. **Some have outlived generations!** Sincerely yours, the **New York Stock Exchange**

started from a coffee shop! Find this out! **This is the reason you have to start from ZERO-CAPITAL business** and map out strategies in your choice business' plan to grow (later consider multi-source of income) of your choice, or that suit your nation/ residential area as demand and tastes differ from a place to another.

2.2 ZERO-CAPITAL BUSINESS IN BRIEF

These are **service rendering business and talents that pave way for developing skills.** They are products of /or sourced from your senses, hobby, interests, turn-on (in addition, some people turn-on and turn—off could trigger the kind of business you can pick interest in) . . . . For such to thrive, it has some ingredients like your **personal humane character, efforts, moral persuasion, social, endurance, patience, prayers and the three T's namely truthfulness, transparency and trustworthiness. Henry Ford** once wrote:*"The two most important requirements for success in business are foresight and patience. And the man who lacks patience lacks the critical quality for success"* Meanwhile, bear it in your mind that your first customers are your family members, residents around you, school ex-colleagues, friends, elder's pals, younger one's pals, relatives, faith-based members, social club members and you continue to build more market share for your product or service. This writer has his first patronage of his books from a connection of a friend in teaching profession to another school. From the school, he met the **P**ublic **R**elations **O**fficer (**PRO**) for a school proprietors/proprietress association of the local government. At the venue, he got formal introduction after a long wait with his products. Some schools immediately picked interest, picked some of the book and they gave the names of their schools and location. The rest is history. In short, the emphasis is that **CREATE FIRST SET OF CUSTOMERS FROM THOSE VERY CLOSE TO YOU AND START EXPANDING THE BASE**.

An additional thing is the expertise advice of the gurus in advertising on how to start promoting the business idea. **Nigeria**'s **Chris Dogudge**, an advertising guru, in his work on advertising, he recommended using **two OPMs** to build one's business. The first is the use of **Other People's Money (OPM1) and Other People's Minds (OPMs 2)**. By **O**ther **P**eople's **M**oney, we do not mean borrowed money or venture capital; we mean 'voluntary disposable money' from their pockets to purchase a good product/service from the business owner. This is never contradictory to the subject matter. Get the explanation right now. You have a good business idea for the people who are seriously yearning for it. Fortunately, these people have money in their accounts and pockets looking for the thing that you have to purchase (being a dire need of theirs) or sponsor (finance) to add value to their wealth. Don't you know that you would get their money in exchange for your idea? Think positively on a product or service (of their interests) that such people would buy at a price from you. This is one of the ways to start big from **O**ther **P**eople's **M**oney even if such is a miser! You do not need to have good credit rating with individuals or financial institutions to get capital to expand what you started small or to get enough money to buy the tools needed or the raw materials. Let us take some instances, a keen fan of a sport should visit academies or open training pitches to discover talents. Let him act as **a broker** to sell the talent on a mutual consent to teams' management (coach/trainers, manager, technical crew, sponsor). Such would make his own money! Help in the recruitment of wanted talents for clubs and get paid for your service! Another instance is the **organizing of events** for the ex-champions in different sports as a broker with good, viable proposals. A financier/promoter would show interest so far the events can pull crowd to make **capital gains**. Imagine featuring 'Iron' **Mike Tyson** with **James Buster Douglas** or **Hulk Hogan** versus **'The Undertaker'** on a non-title bouts or featuring **evergreen singers/creative writers** with the new, or football events for archrival nations or sprints events for aged and retired athletes like **Carl Lewis, Marvin Haglers, Sugar Ray Leonards, Chidi Imohs** . . . Listen, if you think that is too steep to climb, start from broker bouts and contests for local champions in your community! Leave the international ones to **Don Kings** of this world! **Don King** also started small! Baby does not walk the day he is born. I am aware of an artiste who got a sponsor for a film script and both reaped gains at the end of the day! The film was done and sold to an independent marketer for a good price. That is our own view on using **Other People's Money(OPM1)**. Remember *this is not borrowing but selling* (one of the numerous endowments that you possess) to them (target rich clients) in order to get what you need in their (your target clients') pockets which you can neither beg to acquire nor use a force on them to part with.

Really, it is not easy to start with no money at all especially in a nation where all social infrastructure are in shambles, not visible and costly when available! Capital is not there at all even at small interest. But we have to encourage freshers. You need to be encouraged just like this author. Summon courage to get to the top of the mountain. **It is attainable and not a hard task.** It could take vary time for each **job**. You are at great advantage if you already have a skill, talent and interest. The dearth of all facilities to work with is a good challenge as that also paves way to start a brokerage **job** without investing more than your sweat and intelligence. In the course of this research I met a friend who discovered a precious stone site and got a foreign firm from social networking to come and work there with their facilities for a good agreement. As at the moment, all paperwork and inspection had finished and they are only awaiting a court pronouncement to legally back the site and the mining activities commence! This widens your scope to get solutions to myriads of problems and each would fetch both money and honour. If you can withstand the heat at that period, then you will have the last and enduring laugh when things are okay! All successful business gurus in the world employed **cost-saving** to start piecemeal. It took them some years of making their dream a reality. The booster is the focus. Have you got an idea to have a viable business plan of? The noblest among us says: *"No wisdom surpass good planning"*. The first thing in management/administration is to **have a plan.** House is built following a building plan. Vehicles are built based on a building plan. Meals are prepared with a plan on the type and the ingredients. Design one to know the right path to tread. *A journey of one thousand kilometre begins with an ambitious first step*. Never mind about the dearth of infrastructure. At the initial stage, you need not worrying yourself. Never think of the private money lenders or interest-based financial houses, they can help finance your dream business, but the interest rates would kill your business or make you life span servicer of the mounting debts. You should be aware this time that those mentioned common source of finance are out to make money too for life. Unfortunately, banks are getting distressed today and most of them cannot risk their money on a starter like you so you are to find alternative. This is where this book will be a great assistance to you. They would dangle offers with huge incentives to lure you into savings with them but sincerely yours, they cannot lend you a financial assistance to start a new business like yours. No lender would ever tell you this and that is the absolute bitter truth. Many undeveloped nations who have borrowed in the past are still servicing the debts to date yet the debts are increasing every year. They have mortgaged the lives of the unborn generations. Keep this with you in your left palm; **safe money is the money invested in a business of interest.** Ask yourself a few questions: <u>"What is my area of strength? What are my weak points(bear it in mind that your weak points can be worked upon by finding solutions for and be a good source of income, that is, your weak points can give you **job**)? What does my people around and beyond really need at this moment? How do they want it? How populous is the target user? Then, where do I start and with what tools, ingredients, materials and at what time?</u>

Hold this, as you can use **OTHER PEOPLE'S MONEY** as you have been told just as the author of this work (read critically both the preface and acknowledgement over again) and **OTHER PEOPLE'S MINDS**, by sharing your problem to get solutions, so also these: a) **Other people's materials** e.g. idle premises (residence or office), gadgets (electronics, telecommunication . . .) b) **Other people's methods** i.e. techniques or technical knowledge in transfer of technology c) **Other people's machinery** e.g. idle machineries/tools needed for your work like computer, printer, vehicle, generator . . . d) **Other people's markets** i.e. selling in the same business districts/areas/arena before creating yours e) **Other people's managerial skills** among other **OPM's** you could ever think of!

In the course of this work, we will be more concerned with the use of the latter **OPM's** and **<u>not Other People's Money directly</u>** (*emphasis* *mine)*. Let me whisper this into your listening ear again, this writer started from selling a four—page children story for **fifteen thousand naira** (just ninety six American Dollars) which was enough to produce at least **six hundred copies** of another thirty—four page children story with full coloured glossy cover and graphics!. Remember that starting small is from sole proprietorship. Again, to get this material published, it took the investment of a financier, who is convinced about the content acceptability, to pay the publisher simply because the product is right at the right time showing that his returns on capital is sure! Imagine investing some hundreds and reap in thousands! Someone who believes in your products or ideas, even without a penny, would get you a capital provider on a commission or even gratis! It takes a man to dream (hope). Remember **the dream** (hope) of **Martin Luther King (jnr)** about his nation, **America,** has come to pass in the election of **Barrack Obama** as the **first African American President of America**. Dream and reduce your dream into writing, one day, some day, it will come to pass. **Richard Branson and his friends** co-founded **Virgin Atlantic** business, **Bill Gates and Paul Allen** co-founded **Microsoft; Fords, Pembertons, Dells** . . . of this world started from partnership, some as a one-man business. Their ventures were/are appreciated and encouraged by their kinsmen and friends before growing to international companies. That has been the motivating factor they enjoyed that you need too. Sincerely, they all heard that dream of having big corporation and that was the reason when the inspiration to do certain thing came to mind, they grabbed the opportunity from slipping away. My people, in their wisdom, say: *"you should do the acrobatic display behind the stage before you depart for the stage to entertain the audience"*.

2.3 GETTING STARTED WITHOUT FUNDS-PRACTICAL LIFE EXPERIENCE

Although this is discussed in detail in the piece-**'Waste-to wealth jobs'** by the same author(book for copies), let me give you some hints on some ways; you can start with conversion of many valuable things in your possession or control to start your business idea without necessarily be sleepless thinking how to raise funds to take off. **Hear and cudgels your brains over these practical life experience:**

A man of 25, graduated as an apprentice in a welding business. His old parents are poor but have some hectares of lands lying fallow very close to a public institution. The guy started doing some menace **job** to sustain self as he could not get the necessary equipment to start what he learnt. In your view, suggest a solution to his problem as a business consultant.

Another guy is orphaned and a graduate of **Economics** with good grade. He inherited, as his own share from inheritance, a four room wing from his parents' houses. By training in some skills acquirement centre, he is a painter and visual artist by hobby. Counsel him on what to do as he has fruitlessly search for **white/blue collar jobs** for five years.

In short, with the guide in this book, the fear of having millions or thousands to start has been finally rested.

The natural law is that whatever you sow, depending on the soil, climate and nurturing (efforts) will become fruitful and multiplies. *A good seed produces a minimum of ten seeds in harvest*. Invest a shilling, a cent, a kobo ... and be sure of having tens of such. Invest tens and you are sure of reaping in hundreds. Sow hundreds and be sure of harvests in thousands on and on. This is how **Warren Buffets, Bill Gates, Richard Bransons, Fords, Lever Brothers** ... grow to be what they are today. **Dale Carnegie** was a good **motivation speaker** just like **John Foppe**. Meanwhile, it takes a 'blind' with business-mind and who is optimistic of the **Return On (his) Investment (ROI)** to invest hard earned penny! **If you desire to reach the highest, you have to start from the lowest.** Remember that it takes time, steady movement with courage to reach the top of the tallest **Himalaya (Everest) Mountain** from the ground. It is better to be such a wise blind instead of being a pound foolish and pennywise who turns deaf ears to wise business counsel. Daylight starts to break from darkness; you should understand that simple analogy. Keep trying on your choice profession and by the law of the averages, you will soon get a lift!

2.4 LEARN THE ROPES

The rule is simple: Shine your eyes and apply your senses appropriately. The scriptures reveal *"Verily, We created man from a drop of mingled sperm, in order to try him, so We gave him (the gifts) of hearing and sight"*. These are the major senses in the same house-**head, the power station!**You meditate (ruminate) over what you either see or hear. These make you advance to taste, feel or imagine. Only your senses are needed to scout for all those **jobs** you can start without a dime. When I heard a corper's lamentation over **paucity of jobs** for graduates and the skilled including the talented with the effects of unemployment in the nation, this prompted this research work. **How on earth will a graduate staying idle when he can employ his/her professional skill?** We act on what we see and hear. Learn about your immediate needs of your environ to proffer solutions. **A study shows that learning with senses is vital. Learner learns 20 percent by hearing; 30 percent by seeing; 50 percent from apply both hearing and seeing; and 90 percent from acting what you see and hear.** Can you see that the scriptural verse is vindicated! Additionally, all the faculties are: a) Faculty of seeing b) Faculty of hearing c) Faculty of tasting d) Faculty of thinking and e) Faculty of smelling/feeling.

Another scriptural verse reads: *"Many are jinns (spirits) and men We have made for hell: they have HEARTS wherewith they UNDERSTAND NOT, EYES wherewith they SEE NOT, and EARS, wherewith they HEAR NOT. They are like cattle . . ."* Another reads: *". . . and We had endowed them with (faculties of) hearing, sight and heart and intellect . . ."*. Make the optimal use of these faculties altogether to discover your choicest area of interest before you read the next chapter and you have done yourself a great favour and save some cost to get discovered by another person or institute. Sincerely yours, dive within you and **meditate**. Meditate over your hidden personality, your racial background, your own immediate family, personal habit/ interests (hobbies).**Ask yourself** "Which of the stated **hobbies** do I derive ultimate joy and satisfaction? Are you an avid reader with flexible audible voice? Are you a prolific writer? Are you an extrovert? What quality do you have as a unique feature? A business-conscious person puts this and what to give to people to satisfy their need as the first priority and not the money to make. Charity-based organizations brings along with it immeasurable rewards later for volunteers. This reminds me of limitless **volunteer jobs** from the institutions like the **United Nations (UN)**. "Apply as a volunteer if you have a relevant certificate, humanitarian skill, multilingual . . . . You could be called during the crises of nations without pay except some allowances, if you serve the cause diligently and meritoriously, believe me, you will be offered a **JOB** after about a few months of putting in a sincere voluntary service without pay as I am"-This is the voice of admonition from a **United Nations** worker to a friend of mine. By interest, even keeping some domestic pets for fun at home can be turned to money-making business! A good cook at home could make that a profession. Many fast foods joints' (eateries and restaurants) owners today owe their inception to that act! In short, meditate. Meditate over your immediate environ(home, street, village, town, state, region, nation, nations, culture and religion ethics),whatever is their endowment is enough to engage you likewise whatever they lack could render you a way out of joblessness!.

Generally speaking,**some of the JOBS with zero-capital are the service providing JOBS** (Get a copy of **JOBS WITH ZERO CAPITAL VOL.2** by the same author). They are **service-transformation.** Flip over the page and learn. Get the value for the book price. An advice for you is that you should not stay on them for long, make your money and begin to invest on another area of interest. If you can, develop the chosen business into a bigger business for your next generation. We shall research to write how to develop all or most of the highlighted businesses in the next chapter into a big business that give **jobs** for others.

3.1. JOBS WITH ZERO-CAPITAL

1. AGENCY/CONTRACTOR/BROKER/ MIDDLEMAN

Oxford Advanced Learner's Dictionary defines agent as a person who is to act for or manage the affairs of other people in business, politics, etc or a person who is to find work for an actor, musician or to find somebody who will publish writer's work. Such has an important effect on a situation. To make all business grow, for a government policies to be achieved, for peace to return to a warring nation, for a firm to sell all its goods/service to target clients, **all need the service of agents/brokers.** Agency is the intermediary **job** of a middleman or a connector between a searcher of a need and the owner without investing any money but efforts and intelligence. They are independent and self-employed! This is a **job** for all unemployed professionals in different fields. They are everywhere and inevitable, for their services, in all **jobs/services!** They are '**agent of pollination**' or '**agent of change**' It all depends on smartness, experience, prompt application of information and social networking! The searcher can be producers/manufacturers or the buyers. In all the cases, always share the feelings of your clients at both sides, that is, the buyers and the sellers in which you serve as the link.

Agency includes doing the outsourcing **job** for individuals, firms and government. **"Outsourcing,** according to an expert, **Olusoji Oyawoye**, Chief Executive Officer, Resources Intermediaries Limited, Nigeria, is where you transfer the work responsibility**

and the decisions concerning the work of a firm and the staff doing the work to someone outside your business". This is not done in most economies and it is adversely affecting the viability and hence threatening the survival of the businesses. What stops a firm whose warehouse is full to employ independent sales agents to sell to clients across the nation(s)? In case you are not employed to do that, present yourself physically. As an agent, your confidence, fluency, decency and good human relations with people not excluding your **smartness, transparent, truthful, trustworthiness and respectfulness** could earn you big offer. A competent authority (management) through the permission of the owner (entrepreneur) goes for sales agent and the agreement reached would determine the amount the agent can make. Agent should have **good client relation** and very charismatic. 'Many millionaires in **America** are those in selling other people's products and services' **Mr. Brian Tracy** wrote. They are Sales agents/consultants on commission basis, within and outside. Learn more about this agency work you need no dime to start with except your professional qualification and intuitive. Mind you, the aforementioned include those without a paper qualification; they became sales agents/consultants on the basis of their interests. For instance, do you have the idea to sell all the goods in the company XYZ warehouse to particular clients at a location for a good price to sell volumes? If 'yes', then you are on your part to hit it gold! Write the company now because they need you! Such agents are agent of social engineering and that of progress. Both the producers/manufacturers/service providers and the poor talented/skilled ones need them. Listen, most renowned companies across **America** and **Europe** (names withheld) that are applying for bankruptcy need your service (urgently) to expand their distribution channels hence create new markets to bail them out. The problem of running bankrupt is solved if they can get independent agents at strategic locations to sell their wares to enhance profit making as usual. Visit internet to be aware of some of the companies in all sectors! A persuasive proposal from you could give them a relief and earn you big income! Most people who are multimillionaires make it from being an agent! They come across the product/service they sold/are selling to make money from adverts inside prints or the electronic media! Be an independent agent for all businesses/service of your choice. The large the number of businesses and services, the large the number of independent agents for each town especially in a multilingual nation. Read more from the second volume. Before then, learn to know a few of them:

COMMON TYPES OF AGENTS

a) **Estate agent**: Are you in good books of your neighbours? Do you pass the **three T's test?** I mean, are you **truthful, trustworthy** and **transparent**? Then, approach your neighbours to manage their property for them. Not all of them will turn this service down especially if you tell them the advantages of working for them. You will be running this from your room. Collecting registration fees and a percentage of the rentage/lease of lands, houses, offices, malls . . . under your control. You will end up becoming big estate manager dealing in real estate business, helping your clients buying and selling of property! Take for instance, if you shop for potential clients to get good houses at choice locations, get in touch with the help of your social connection (people) to get buyers/renters/lease holders and your commission is awaiting you after the deal. Search for property for sale from the established firms, compile them and employ your links to get buyers/renter. Do not be idle if you are a graduate of **E**state **M**anagement, **B**uilding **T**echnology, **C**ivil **E**ngineering, **A**rchitecture . . . Apply your professional knowledge wisely and positively! In all cases again, put yourself in the shoes of both. Ensure you critically look at the property before it is offered for purchase/rentage/lease and occupant/sale. This adds value to your integrity and trustworthiness. If you have the links, you are a promising **realtor**! Develop it gradually to reach the real height where you rightly belong (worthy of).

b) **Job/employment agent:** Aborigines and the people who are looking for **jobs** especially the emigrants need agents. This serves as a link between the employers and the employees. Sincerely yours, you are helping both sides by reducing costs for them! Graduates in **Sociology** and social sciences, this is a good **job** for you. Be friendly to personnel departments of organizations to get the vacant slots and requirements. With good negotiation and conviction, the company will spare part of procurement cost with you while you are still entitled to a percent in the salaries of the eventual employees. You have reduced costs of advertisement and procurement processes incurable by the employers and the costs of getting suitable **jobs** by the prospective employees! What you need to do are: make efforts to meet **P**ersonnel **O**fficers/**M**anagers or owners of sole proprietor businesses, demand for vacant posts, the remuneration, the expected workload for the employees whose positions are vacant, briefs about the companies/businesses to have an in-depth look about the future and opportunities ahead both parties . . . Open 'office' in your home, your garage, parlour or even rest-room, or your close pal/friend's office after reaching agreement. Advertise the **jobs** on a board (use to coach your wards at home) with chalk. You will see floods of the idlers in dire need of the **jobs.** Collect registration fees based on the nature of **jobs**; agree on percentage from the salary/remuneration before taking them to the employers. Advancement in this course would end you becoming a corporate procurement company and consultant like **Schlumberger** and **Phillip Consulting**! The latter also started moving up the ladder gradually.

c) **Travelling/tours agent:** Unemployed History, tourism management graduates and related courses have landed themselves in **jobs** if they desire to make it from tourism business. Just like the next form of agency below. The only difference is that as a travelling agent, you lead vehicles, ships . . . to their destinations. You should be hence being exceptional in map and compass reading. Update your knowledge if you desire this kind of **job**! School pupils who go for periodical excursion need your service. This is an all year round business as far as the number of schools is concerned! Manufacturers of goods in particular, especially those new investors in your country/state/province/village, need your service. You are employed with your driving skill as a sales representative. To them, you are the grassroot man that can help them get accomplished! In the absence of manufacturers, to get commonest patronage, start with school owners well known to you. Their eventual recommendations to other schools would help you gain more clients hence more income!

d) **Tourists agent**: For you that have little formal education, imagine a man born and bred in a neighbourhood full of tourist attraction centres. He is fortunate that the centres have been recognised by **UNESCO.** Unfortunately, this man is looking for **job** in the city whereas **tourism** in his village is enough to fetch him big money! Kindly relocate and get more knowledge about all those **sites,** learn to understand and speak some major dialects (multilingual) and you have got what it takes to be a good tourists' agent. Visitors, researchers or tourists are coming to employ your services to enjoy their stay! The **Arabs** and those who understand the language make big sums of money during the months of Holy pilgrimages for pilgrims outside **Arab** world.

e) **Raw-material agent**: This is **Job** for you those of you that studied **P**urchasing and **S**upply, **M**arketing and related courses. Apply your professional knowledge. Get all your information about products and services (for production) with cheap internet service with your mobile set affordable from the stipend saved from your daily basic allowances! Assume **company ABC** is in need of a raw material 'x' and you are aware of the source/producer of the material. Send your proposals to both as a supplier to the one in need and as distributor for the second. Agree to pay (to your supplier) for the material after receiving the payment from your buyer. The amount you spend on the proposals is from your nest egg. Just as some people are looking for **jobs**, some factories, old and new, are in dire need of raw materials at cheaper rates. Do you aware of a place of what and what is sold in large quantity with a cheaper price to the prevalent prices? If you have the passion for selling and supplying, then you are a foot away to get engaged. Just think what Company/individual 'A' needs and how it is needed, get information on the producers of the need and lastly compare the price with the disposable income of those in need. It costs you zero–equity and part of your **nest egg**. Then, **shopping for them** is a good **job** that costs you nothing but good approach and well designed agreement for your remuneration after or before service! Start from a company well known **but** who will pay for your service. Present **proposals** to others showing how you helped your first client to procure their raw materials and expect patronages!

f) **Educational agents**: These are 'foreign' schools' representatives. You can be a representative of a school in your country in a region of that country. You act as admission agent for the school for an agree fees/commission. Education Managers and Counsellors by profession, where are you? Your inevitable service **job** abounds virtually every corners of the land. The reason is as a result of the essentialities of education. A maxim says: '*He who says that education is costly should try ignorance*'. After all, **the noblest** was reported to have said: '*He who desires the life of this world should seek for knowledge, he who desires of the next world should seek for knowledge and he who desires both should seek knowledge*'. In another he says: '*Seeking knowledge is a must for males and females*' and '*Seeking knowledge is from cradle to grave*'. *Womb to tomb,* of course hence the need to establish schools to seek knowledge everywhere legitimate. Many with desire for a particular knowledge need to be guided to where such is established. Those with raw talents need schools where they can be properly fine-tuned. Education agents' work in this regard is inevitable. Can you pick an appointment for a school to be their representative in your region where such lacks and in dire need of one? Start small, get enrollees for schools for a fee to start with, you will end up becoming an accredited agent of many schools!

g) **Scouts/sports agents**: As large as sports talents abound, then opportunities for games masters, trainers, admirers, and those who studied relevant courses to excel in picking up this **job**. Do you watch athletes and sportsmen in contests and practices to discover talent for sale? Do not just watch for fun. Watch to discover new talents in all positions. Many sports clubs need certain area/vacuum to fill. Get this vacuum filled from getting a right person(s) for them to get incomes. The vacuum is a need to be filled. Emulate **Ross Perot**, a former salesman of **IBM** who saw and filled a need (handling of data processing needs) for his customers when his employer rejected the idea. His own **Electronic Data**

Processing eventually founded was later sold for **$2.8 billion** to **General Motor!** With this he made his billions and became one of the richest in history! Again, looking at football, imagine the amounts being generated by football agents/scouts across the world! What about publishers of biographies of distinguished personalities in all fields, poetry, songs, books, diaries, memoirs into hardcopy, audio book and e-product/service(s)? Be an agent of a particular talent or skill. Advertise and get submissions. Enter necessary agreements with those talented ones or their representatives and you have launched yourself into a limelight. This gives thousands of **jobs** opportunities if adequately explored. It is simply a **leisure/pastime job** towards discovering, nurturing and promoting talents. Without this, many talents will return to soil unexplored and hence fruitless (waste).

h) **Artistes/artist/musician agents:** The last lines in the above have explained it all. Talents need discoverers, nurturers and promoters to come into good use. In fact, Our Creator is so merciful that talents are naturally bestowed on creatures to turn round the world. They are tools for social interaction and development. In a limitless way, talents play inevitable role in the **social engineering** of the world. Becoming an agent, a link between the owners and the users of those talents is a **natural job.** One can even say that that (discovering; nurturing; promoting) is a talent too!

i) **Mobile money agents:** In a Developing nation like **Nigeria,** this is a new **job** waiting to be explored by indigenous entrepreneurs and the foreigners. A **job** that will reduce financial crime rates enhances business efficiency, production process and primarily gives **jobs** for many professionals from different specialisations. Imagine the numbers that will be needed across the nation. For those without capital to start in this case, they are the people locating very close to the people like the stationed phone booth owners. **Mobile Money Agent Companies** licensed need the latters' services for a fee to be their representatives to advert and other engagements. Alternatively, you can become one in the front of your house depending on your location! Get a well-packaged proposal to the licensed to be aware of how your location would help the growth of their business and expect a huge patronage! They will provide all what you need to erect a suitable office just as good locations attract manufacturers to select some merchants as their sole distributors!

j) **Courier/information and communication technology agents:** Just like the above, locate very close to market places/ business districts/government secretariats/industrial estates or layouts/housing estates will surely help you becoming a good agent for all those companies. They too are looking for a way to reduce the costs of transportation and delivery (distribution) so your location is enough to attract them to your proposals to become their agent! Try your luck with your professional experience. You could become **press agent, postal agent, agreement agent, box office agent** . . . for a negotiable fee. Make some proposals from the savings from daily sustenance fees. If you have the interest, start now!

k) **Liaison officers/firms (technical/marketing/sales)/ association agents:** This simply means: be a **P**ublic **R**elation **O**fficer especially if you are a senior citizen. Your reputation would speak for you. (Read extensively from **'jobs for the retirees and the aged'** written by the same author). This reminds me of my business interaction with a friend who just established a cyber café. His major problem was how to get clients. I decided to become his agent when I saw his disinterest in ways to win customers. What did I intend to do? I will bargain for all the services for a price, locate schools, offices and other places to get bulk works for him. For instance, he was doing on-line registration for Two Hundred naira. It was bargained at one hundred and fifty naira per head as an agent. I believe I will be able to win the hearts of some headmistresses and proprietors of at least forty schools for a commission of twenty naira per head. I target about two thousand pupils-fifty pupils per school. Thirty naira per head would fetch me, the agent, **Sixty Thousand Naira!** Imagine if my social connections help me mass photocopying, lamination, spiral binding and shopping on-line for a few organizations. I will be making **Hundreds of Thousand Naira per month**. Later, I would be able to start my own business centre!

l) **Broker services in marketing of other's products and services:** This is also a **major zero capital business.** Another good example is Stock broking, insurance broking, peace/conflict broker, advertising agents . . . even talent brokers! Again, a **broker** makes this work become published with a good **return in returns** for his brokerage service! Simply put, it is broad and cheap to do especially for those who have special qualifications. More are specially packaged in the **second volume** of this work titled: **Jobs with zero—capital (vol.2)**

"Listen attentively
If you have neither talent nor skill
But you have social connections
That social resource could make you rich
Provided you become a broker for the poor talented/skilled"

N. B. For enquiries and more guides, mail to latlib222@yahoo.com/ writer's facebook)

Let us refresh before we proceed on the subject of discussion. Learn about some additional needed inputs to get all of the above effectively done.

ADDITIONAL INPUTS NEEDED

These are the additional needed inputs for making success of any chosen **zero-capital job** aside the **three T's-Truthfulness, Transparency and Trustworthiness**(ensure you find the three in the owner and your client to safeguard working with or for a crook), and the three P's of success-**Patience, Perseverance and Prayers** already discussed:

a) `**INFORMATION**: This is the first and the most useful thing needed to be a good self-employed person. You must have fresh and genuine information (hard facts and figures) about your line of business and the data must be updated to be an effective self-employed. For an estate agent-to-be for instance, you need timely information to secure the right of the owner of property, job, data, location, cost of rentage, market value, period of lease, agreement deed, legal procedure, ... Acquiring all relevant information to enable your business to grow is the first assignment. After establishing yourself, getting information about the needs of clients and the business environment is essential.

b) **PACKAGING**: You should be able to package yourself to get a buyer of your service. The way you dress, they say, is the way you would be addressed. Based on the type of service you are intended to render for a fee, watch your manner of dressing, comportment and appearance generally. A good chef in search of hotelier or food canteen owner to give employment to should look smart and neat. All cleaning service **jobs** require a neat handler. This reminds me of a man that usually dressed in different designers to have his usual seat in a reception of a popular hotel, many of the clients to the hotel showed admiration to the designers having been noted. Some walked to him to chat with him. They sought to know his designer which he claimed to be the seller of the fabrics and the designs were being done in his workshop by his designers. This won him some supplies for the customers he created from the hotel and that was the beginning of his raising capital to start his dream fashion business (company) from being a tailoring contractor!

In today's world, we have heard of one-man singer, drummer, actor, comedian . . . even self-publisher!

c) **DYNAMISM**: You should be dynamic and not rigid. Old method might not work for you as it worked for others, in the same/similar business, before you. A strategy that made wonder in a nation might be a failure if applied in another, so be dynamic. Always reflect on how best to present your service to your target clients. Let me cite an instance of a man from a drummer family, if you are a type that is introvert and selective in the wake of visiting social events, then it may be huge task to sell your innate **job** for buyers to patronize. You must become a social person who should be an extrovert overnight. Meanwhile, you must set a target for yourself hence you grow towards the right line. Those who started with nothing or little had targets. This is what you intend to achieve or to have become in certain years ahead. Be dynamic and work vigorously towards achieving your aim. Hunter aims at his prey to conquer in the forest. They grow their business gradually. I know of a man whose trade is to sell latest fashion trends in masculine dress to visitors at a popular hotel. Many admirers walked to him to enquire where and who designed the dress, he gave them his business cards personifying self as the designer and material seller. He got a lot of contracts where he made his first one hundred thousand naira gain in a year! The man shopped for the material, gave them to his designers with all the measurements from his clients. Can you start a business like that without investing a dime but your intelligence, politeness and efforts?

d) **CREATIVE:** This is doing a new thing or dynamism to make a difference. You have to consider competitors in the market, existing or potential entrants. They are your rivals that will help you to be on your feet. If you want to stay long in business, you must be able to create new trends before the expiration of one. Be unique and always be innovative. Come out with new ideas in that line of business to beat or be distinct at least from others. Script writers of films; write two-cast, three-cast, four—cast, five—cast . . . films with short, medium and long durations. For every product or service, something is missing; find it and produce something better and unique! Introduce new dimension to an existing product or service to make a new thing. I tell you, if we have a million existing **jobs;** you should be able to create another million, at least if you are so creative! (Read **'New jobs from the existing jobs'** by the same author) A religious person should be religiously inclined to set up a **job.** For instance, a Muslim/puritan script writer and film producer should produce men—only (actors) film and women—only (actress) films with inscription on the jacket 'for Muslim women only' simply because women voices are naked! Such should use costumes that are allowed in Islam to get patronage and not condemnation. Aside that every prospective entrepreneur should be able to identify the needs of people such as social, economic, spiritual, technological, political . . . He should then tailor his **job** activities towards that to set up.

e) **SOCIAL NETWORK:** No business idea can grow to the anticipated level at the expected pace without <u>social networking</u>. It is a major ingredient in marketing success. No clients could be got without adequate social networking. Advertisements no matter how fancy and alluring, you must have good and quality mode of networking to win the hearts of target clients. You need clients from your family and friends to take off smoothly. This starts from your immediate family members, then friends—intimate or pen pal like friends on social sites, ex-colleagues at schools, associates, and neighbours! Those are your non-commissioned publicists. The only way a foe, near or far, will help you is to speak the truth about your performance (strength and weak points) or your product quality. This is not envy as both comments will help you to live up to expectation and rebrand. Just imagine yourself as a fashion designer, you are to be in charge of the wardrobes of the family of six and you got paid, imagine the income for your business to grow!. This is about publicizing your business to people through people, to a family through the mothers or their children. Take for instance, if you are good in traditional plaiting of hair and you are very **creative** in the **job**, if you 'enter' through a daughter, her mother may join as one of your clients. She will surely introduce you to another family in the neighbourhood. This is how your business of plaiting would spread to hundreds of family that home service would not be able to manage again but a big shop in the neighbourhood! Never you forget using all affordable social media like **facebook, twitter, YouTube, LinkedIn,** mobile adverts, advert—on—line, websites, on-line stores, bulk short message service aside man to man, neighbour to neighbour, place to place. Never rely solely on your marketers' intuitiveness alone, create new market strategies with the exploration of the **social sites!** Visit individual websites based on their specializations to sell the skills/talents you have discovered. Tell coaches, artistes' promoters, publishers, film/documentary producers, boards of organizations even government owned websites! **Social networking** is a good source of boosting clients' base and making money without investing a dime. It is simply a **broker service** that can provide **jobs** for thousands! Take this simple analogy: If a nation registered 10,000 businesses and all of them employ an external sales agent per state in a 36–state nation. Such would have 36 x 10,000 sales agents total 360,000 direct **jobs and triple sale assistants**. Imagine if they all have agents for all towns with a target sales volume, what could be the number of **jobs** (direct and indirect) created and the multiplier effect on income distribution to millions of dependants and the returns on investments for the companies/organisations? A friend, Mubak Woodwork Technology and Furniture Maker used to buy credits daily to call/invite clients to visit his showroom and for getting/securing new **jobs/contracts**. I am also in the habit of making 70 percent of my credits on business related calls. This is social networking when you cannot reach all the people/clients at distances apart face to face. When I finished writing this work, I browsed to get publishers abroad where they have very good reading culture clients. Having known that the work would be a commercial success there, I discussed with several publishers after studying their profiles before settling for this publisher!

f) **PRICING:** At initial stage, you must be moderate and considerate in giving price for your service to your clients. Sometimes high price distinguishes buyers as it could be an attraction for the rich and chase away the poor from patronage. High price could turn some unserious away even if you give the best service. Some value quantity than paying for quality. Sometimes, let your client pay intentional price for the good service rendered and do not be surprised to have a customer who would surprise you by paying more than you could have demanded for! If my advice will be an absurdity, do not charge or take money for your service for the **first jobs** done and you are assured of big patronage the moment you announce that you have taken the **job** as a business. Your **quality job** would fetch you more than your official charge soon with time (patience).

g) **Prudence**: A business—minded person should be modest in spending. This writer was into what they called '**Bootstrapping**' when he started his publishing business. He started small with funds from three friends who believed in his talent of researching/writing. He made some sales and continued to re-invest the accruals till he had enough to produce nine titles and several research works which include this! What the educational books cannot fetch him in years, this work would do in a couple of months. Any doubt? This method will help a fresh starter to learn practical money management and wise in investing unlike someone who started with a big sum of capital. It is hence advisable to *start a business with zero-capital and zero-equity.* Well, extravagance is wasting the available financial and time resources in particular. You should spend both very wisely in a way to bring back a rewarding return for your investment. Never mind being called a non-socialite or a miser. Every penny is invaluable to an entrepreneur. You should be able to separate the resources for other spending from the one for the business. Be prudent in managing your financial and other resources. Aside that, study the peak period of your business. **Never you play around (idle) at business peak periods**. Time determines the rise and fall of a business. Punctuality, dedication, passion, discipline consistency are some of the good principles of any successful business. If you decide to earn a salary for your initial efforts, let the business pay your salary/wage. Pay yourself 10% of the total income as monthly salary and then invest the rest just as "**The Richest Man in Babylon**" so written by **George Classon**. Create a **financial independent account** where you continue to keep it. If you cannot, ensure you spend within your salary but make a certain percent saving for the rainy day (future investments) monthly! **Separate business from charity**. Business is profit-centred and not charity-oriented except the annual **Business Social Responsibility** from the yearly net gains! This, if done, will promote/improve your business **goodwill**. Never invest blindly on another business you lack information about even from your monthly savings. **Never be a penny wise, pound foolish.** Remember that **an infinite numeral starts from a unit.** A wisely invested kobo or cent would soon become a naira or a dollar! Recall again that this writer set a focus for himself when he started. The first revenue he got was re-invested on new products (books). Today, he has nine books to his credit aside the invaluable researched-based manuscripts like this. Avoid playing yourself into a crook's devilish tracks. Do not be extravagant, covetous and greedy. Separate business from relationship. <u>Treat business as an entity and a creation that must outlive the owner</u>. Create a foundation later for the gains of the business to multiply itself and support the foundation till eternity. **Learn** from mentors and those who have set up similar business before you. Establish business relationship with them. Therefore, shine your eyes and apply your senses always! Lastly, **be prudent with TIME.** Once a time is lost on vanity, it is regretted and lost forever! Your **business is like a seed** to a farmer, create time, make sacrifices and consult widely to nurture it to fruition.

h) **Mentoring**: Every new entrant should have an enthusiast and highly experienced humane selfless mentor. A selfless mentor guides his student to know the pros and cons of a chosen career. His life experience will surely help the new entrant. In fact, it is advisable for any prospective entrepreneur to have **a role model in a mentor** who he/she should be consulted at the time of need. Money cannot buy experience. **Chief Ponju Amonri** (of blessed memory), founder of **Vantage Publications,** mentored this writer into developing his art of writing to a money making venture. Along the way, he turned deaf ears and blind eyes to those people around him that were discouraging him about going into self-publishing. With **crowd funding** (tokens) at the first stage from three friends to produce the first publication, today (as at the moment of compiling this piece) **four** of his books are in the supplementary list of **Oyo State Ministry Of Education, Nigeria (2008-2014)** and one is about to be published abroad by a publisher with over ninety years in publishing business. The path to success is very steep and slippery, hold heart and face the challenge. It is a mountain you can reach its peak from the bare ground with courage. Just build on a solid foundation, invest your time, effort and the initial revenue from the little sales wisely to expand gradually!

i) **Professionalise the choice job**: From the inception, never take the job as a mere pastime. Devout your precious time to its growth. People at the end will shower encomiums on you if successful. The business is a seed that must be well nurtured to be fruitful (success). New entrants are coming in as they have seen you as a mentor. Therefore, you must always present yourself as a professional though you **start from home-office.** Sincerely yours, many consultancy firms convert the home facilities into office asset when there is no dime to acquire and furnish an office! Set (arrange) the 'office' like a real office to the taste of your anticipated clients. Your mobile set as your mobile office. Be courteous and ensure that you enter vital information and data about your clients in a data in a neat notebook and ensure you get a monetary reward for that service. The clients will surely take you serious. No client values an indecent and uncultured business owner. See your business as your employer; serve it diligently as a good employee! Never have any fear of falling, many business owners that have made it in history fell sometimes but learn from the fall to rise again!

2. TRADITIONAL HEALING

This includes chanting of legitimate incantations that can heal wounds and poisonous bites and intake poisons. Some incantations are done to wade off evil/spiritual attacks. Never wade off evil with evil. It takes a ray of light to shame darkness. Scriptural knowledge to heal ailment could fetch you in return big sum if done gratis in particular! Alternatively, some are naturally gifted in the use of leaves, herbs, barks of trees, shrubs, epiphytes . . . sap from the barks and the roots of trees/herbs to cure different types of human diseases. This innate knowledge should not be left to waste. The Almighty would see the gifted that does not make the economic and social use of it as a mere waster who does not value good things. Today, in **China, Nigeria, Vietnam** and many other nations, people who are so gifted in the use of herbs and animals for certain healing are reaping in millions as a good alternative to orthodox medicine! The noblest among us says: **'There is no disease without its cure'.** Many in the villages, riverside areas and creeks have the knowledge of medicinal and nutritious herbs to heal all major diseases; it takes courageous graduates to transform this into money-making ventures. In **Nigeria** and many third world nations, many sick rely on herbs to cure their ailments. Unfortunately, plants are not planted as replacements. Over **90%** in **Nigeria** are on herbs without replanting them according to **International Institute of Tropical Agriculture (IITA) Ibadan, Nigeria**! Herbal technology is open to all to explore to the fullest. **Chinese are earning billions of Yens from this technology today**. Get me clear, they are in the brains of the aged and the middle aged in your village; tap the resources before they bid the world farewell even to sell to those pharmaceutical companies here or there!

In addition, creatures in water (**almost 75% of the universe)** are there to be explored for human use. Largest number of creatures in different species dwells inside seas for consumption and medicare of ailments. Probably, the curative drugs to the terminal diseases are in waters if recognition is given to the **Nori tribe** in **Japan, Dulse in coastal Europe** and the **Limu Palahalaha** in native **Hawaiians cuisine** who use seaweeds to cure heart related diseases! Venture into **water technology** and you have buyers for your discoveries in prints or documentaries!

3. COLLECTIONS

Do you have natural flair in collecting of things like stories, events and objects for future use or reference? It pays a good price for you as a collector. It only takes your time. Remember the greatest reward you get for your efforts is not what you get for them but what you become by them. Collection is researching that will raise you to the podium of honour just as **Ali Mazrui** is doing in history! Can you collect information about the history of ancient empires/towns/nations/civilizations/tourist centres; creatures like plants (medicinal and ornamental), animals, birds and other physical creatures on the crust (lands and inside the waters)? The collections can be published as books for researchers and general readers or scripted into documentaries and films. You should however be wary of crooks among the practitioners. Your intellectual work is inestimable as it gives you royalties for many generations. Have you heard that? Your work shall outlive your generation! Listen to these advices, never release your work for review before payment and if you are a commissioned collector, get advance part payments in the beginning, when you get to the middle stage and at the moment of delivery. Just be ready to part with a simple synopsis. This is a very demanding job that takes all the inputs discussed in the course of this book. Go over them again and again as they are your guides to start up your own business. You need to make more research to get more of such but take a particular area of interest in the sub-headings below to maximally use your time:

a) **Collecting of the stories of the legends**:

Every nation has one legend or the other, male or female, young or old, dead or alive. They are the elder statesmen. Some are business moguls. They live in all ages. Immortalise the names of the dead legends by research and write about them. You have started the road to success.

Collecting of stories about the living legends is celebrating the person alive. Collecting his/her story after his/her demise is post-humous celebration. The former would fetch you more fame and honour than the latter for you. What about the stories about your alma mater or your club/society? Your efforts are never in vain as monetary reward always follows fame and honour from launchings provided you best apply your social resources. The legends can be of politics, economy, traditional warriors, ancient writers/educationists, elder statesmen, renowned kings and queens, excelled sportsmen ... Such must have certain traits that made them rose to the category of a legend. As man could be legends, so also are some towns, existing or defunct, some nations have certain historical background that makes such legends. Collect them and go to the film/movie producers within or on internet. Some plants especially **medicinal emigrant plants** and **animals,** the **oceans and streams** with different ancient tales as per origin, **healing power** (other uses) and sources. Imagine the number of legends among all the creatures on the planet earth!

b) **Collecting folklores**:

Based on our social research, hardly would you see in **Africa** an ethnic that does not have some folklore songs to educate and entertain their young ones and adults at a particular season or time. Some have tales under the moonlight to teach morals and pass traditional mores to the target listeners. Look, you don't need to travel to countryside before you get them as rural–urban migration has done the magic for you. Make yourself available to your aged people very close to you and then the relatives, neighbours and start collecting the folklore songs. They are materials for music industry for amusements and publication/ acting in series for kiddies' television slots in animation. The latter can be commercialized as in producing in compact disks for public patronage later. Selling some collated folklore songs to established promoters to produce animation films for kids and adults, to start your own production should be your focus as this writer did to start his publishing business locally!

c) **Collecting of ancient jokes/fable:**

Folklores are different from jokes. The former teaching traditional piece aim at educating the listeners the cultures and moral values whereas jokes is mostly for amusements and not necessary to teach a moral. Yet, many comedians today would need some of your jokes to package him/her self for better patronage. Rather, get this clear, most comedians too are graduates of different disciplines who take to comedy to sustain themselves. My advice is that you too should package yourself for the **one-man show** at events. Brace up for the challenge to be **a star comedian**. Never forget to be social and do your social network to get patronage! People like jokes as it is a remedy to many physiological and psychological diseases. **To start small,** you can start from entertaining schools during events, individuals at social events and then organization before you standby facing large audience in theatre. Just as the standby comedians today, they started from somewhere even at attending show that no penny was paid. Chat with them and learn from their experience as mentor. There are superstitious fables that correct morals through creation of fears into the minds of the listeners, get them collated and approach a publisher to become comics. (Contact latlib222@yahoo.com/writer's facebook for dialogue and guides)

d) **Collecting of history:**

History is a broad and illuminating subject. It could be one of the first natural subjects as it reckons with time and time is eternal. Think of the **history** of all the species among the creatures on and above the soil. **Archaeologists** need your work of history about towns and the foremost inhabitants for the soil exploration for artefacts. History points to what, when, where, which and why. **History is a pointer that guides all knowledge seekers**(biologists, chemists, physicists, pharmacists, journalists, technologists, administrators, accountants, lawyers, surveyors, economists . . .) to do their academic and official researches, so your efforts to collect stories is so invaluable. This is also collecting diary, day to day, event by event as a **ghost writer**. It pays more to collect those of generous celebrities!

e) **Collecting of ornaments, fashion and styles:**

One of the ornaments in mind include those of animals as pets (rabbit, cats, dogs, parrots, peacocks . . .) and plants that are pests flushers. You can get ornamental animals as gifts from breeders and you can start rearing them for commercial purpose. Remember rabbits eat certain grass just as domestic animals. Also, people like fashionable wears from head to toe. A collator of different fashionable materials like beads, chains, textiles of different ethnics get a very large patronage. A typical well travelled **African** woman in **Nigeria** like interest in wearing **'kente'** of **Ghana** no matter the cost. **Yoruba** women who married an **Igbo** husband would not want to look odd in the wives' union so she would prefer dressing in **Igbo** styles of dresses. This is enough as a good reason for collecting different styles and creative designs of fabrics of different ethnic groups for designers. Remember that the designers need such work of yours to make them relevant and remain in business. Collect them under different labels and reach a printing business agreement with a publisher. Both of you will reap profits from working together if you are both trustworthy! Meanwhile, you can also be a middle man, if you can explore the internet, between the buyer and the supplier of different **African** fabrics. Develop this and you could end up become an importer and exporter of fabrics in a short time! Remember a sacrifice (nest egg) from your feeding expenses to browse and send message is the fund needed. Start from selling to family members, trusted colleagues and relatives first before you add to your customers. What about collections of precious stones, sands, marble, granite especially their locations? The latter would land you a big contractual agreement with those dealing in them! (For more guides, mail to latlib222@ yahoo.com/writer's facebook).

f) **Collecting of flowers:**

Flowers are aesthetics for a beautiful environment. Collect ornamental flowers for horticulturists. A collection of white flowers, of good scent, would fetch you love and money from the **Chinese**. Never show them red as it means death and could incur the wrath! Hotels, schools, individuals and corporate organizations are always in need of flowers as ornaments of their premises. Some faiths have even attached so much spiritual importance/value to gathering of scenting and coloured flowers for religious rites. Some are even medicinal in value to cure ailments. In marriage packs, flowers are inevitable from the outset of courtship to the altar! In most countries today as a result of the effect of climate change, governments are investing so much in beautification of streets with flowers and trees! Believe me, just like birds, animals, plants and men, some flowers have migrated to your nation, search for them for commercial purpose!

g) **Collecting of artefacts:**

Artefacts are ancient things that told us about our past. We intentionally did not mention the idols in our lands but ancient interesting events. An old person likes recycling of stories/recycled stories, events and history as refresher and the young generation like to learn from the experience of the elders that lived in the past. This is the reason why the recycled and recycling stories will be hot cake in print and electronics! Such could be myths or real life stories of a great personality. Imagine quoting the legendary of the past on a particular issue. Imagine reporting an interesting football event in human history or **the thrilla in Manila** or **'the rumble in the jungle'** of **Joe Frazier** (of blessed memory) and **Mohammad Ali, the greatest**, in former **Zaire** in **Africa!** Can you recall the hey days of **Mike Tysons** on the ring? Any documentary with his consent to back that up, you producers? What about the life and time of the elder statesmen of your nation or other nations? Remember internet has made the world a village where you can make little efforts to get what you need at a very cheap cost!

h) **Collecting of traditional science and technology:**

Traditional technology includes all art of collecting knowledge of medicinal herbs, barks of plants and their extracts to cure diseases. Many a shrub has its usage that people do not know. There are countless of such knowledge with different ethnic group. What is eating as a vegetable in a town is used as drug-making raw materials in another not forgetting the saying that **'one man's food is another man's poison'**. **Africa** is losing most of the illiterate (in learning western civilization from western form of education) aged people are dying of terminal diseases and hunger in most cases. To preserve these useful local scientific facts that even contain solution for spiritual attacks, somebody must deem it fit to collate all the traditional powers for the benefits of humanity. **No knowledge is a waste.** If such is not useful to human race, it would never be revealed to them at all by the **Creator!** The explorers of **Africa** settled in it to get closer to natural knowledge. They were successful as the knowledge is being transformed into many today's sciences and technology. The established herbal practitioners, local and foreign, are in need of such materials from you for a good pay. It takes some efforts to locate the aged and some moral suasion to get what you need. Ensure you have not less than fifty herbs to heal a disease. Place this on internet in your profile and you will get calls from the practitioners. The research they supposed to do have been done by you! (Refer to compilations about soil, water, herb, air . . .technologies from the traditionists). Remember that some thrive in space technology and astrology. Some of the knowledge reside with many ethnic groups, get them and make money from it

i) **Collecting of proverbs, idioms, quotes and words:** The sole purpose of doing all these is to work towards producing a compilation that will produce ethnic dictionaries for different classes among your ethnic group or others around. Remember that **Europeans** wrote dictionaries for many tribes in the world (even for the **Semitic** race) likewise ancient stories of many nationalities. It is a work of research that is very challenging but eventually highly rewarding both in cash and reference. Nothing stops you from embarking in this project to occupy yourself and for the use of generations unborn. Start collecting them, write them down in black and white, typeset and forward your well packaged proposals or use any of the major ways you have been taught under the **FAQs** as publishers (of e-books and audio-books for e-libraries, laptops ... and paperback) are in need to produce local dialects dictionaries that would contain the proverbs, wisdom of elders in **quotes, idioms, figures of speech and meanings of words and their usage!**

j) **Collections of vacancies containing the types of jobs, qualifications, names of firms, location and news about people, events, breaking news f**or media houses and publishers. This writer has done this many times without numbers for many idlers in search of **jobs** from reading a piece of story! Many regular readers at vendors' joints do not read between the lines to identify those vacant slots. Many a news being read has the capacity to provide **jobs with zero capitals** for the readers but they are ignorant of it! (read the another irresistible title from the same author titled: '**waste to wealth jobs**' for broad knowledge and understanding)

k) **Collections of scraps from firms, factories for recyclers** (remember most firms see you as a helper helping them to dispose their wastes!) This effort will rid the streets of filths and epidemics become a history aside perks that you will collect after delivery to the target buyers/recyclers!

l) **Collection of health, sports, entertainments, memorable quotes and quotable quotes, maxim, proverbs, business tips, tourist centres, historical sites and guides** just as you collect/romance love tips for the people in information and communication technology industry to buy for sale to the interested phone users!

m) **Collection of specialized tips** for public consumption for instance, collecting simple tips guiding the unemployed to search and secured **jobs**; behaviour during and after interview; how to handle challenges in offices; treatment of **job** stress; home stress; motivations; how to treat business failure; treatment of sickness . . . . Take the latter for instance, to treat an addict of either alcohol or cigarette, take **three steps** namely: send reminders to him/her at intervals the evils surrounding taking them, reasons to stop the addiction or taking it in minutest, and after stopping, appreciate such steps he(addict) has taken through the use of texts.

n) **Collection of scriptural lessons for the co-religionists to patronize**. There are faith-based publishing and electronic producing companies who have interest in your efforts. Keep this in your mind; sports, entertainment and religion are the highest money—making ventures across the globe! Remember that you could become a script writer and socio-economic researcher and start at that small stage like this writer!

o) **Collection of stamps**: *This is what they call philately in communication business. The collection and study of stamps. Collectors of used stamps would sell them later at a higher price even as much as ten times the original price of such stamps. The reason being that old stamps publicise history, culture, anniversaries, civilizations, arts and many other information. In a nutshell, collecting stamps only demand time of the collector and the **job** has economic value.*

Mind you, only the times to collect all the mentioned things consume time, your package and the use of any or all the major ways to start apply in all.

'Collectors are doing so with passion
Stories, folklores, histories . . . collected can be entered into prized contests
Winning prize is enough to start your own publishing business or
investment on your works!
Not forgetting the other materials being collected
Buyers of all the materials are available
Just compile or converge
Ask the professionals and producers (users)
Scavenging is no sin, just be decent and polite
In searching you discover new things
A good business is it!'

4. SORTERS

From the name, sorters are those people who have passion for sorting things (materials) out for further recycling. To a sorter, **no thing lying idle is a waste**. They are valuable resources that are convertible again for another product to emerge for use. The lifecycle of all materials follow natural order (law) the cycle continues. **Man goes back to soil his original source likewise all materials**. Materials that are sorted include the rubber/plastics, steel, aluminium, paper wrappers. All these are used as packs or finishing materials for building. (Read more in another piece titled **'Waste to wealth jobs'** by the same author). **Make a booking for copies for you and friends' home libraries**. For further enquiries from the author/researcher, call or send your SMS to: **+234803 215 5018, +234805 671 0944 or mail latlib222@yahoo.com)**

"Sorting is a big deal
An advanced step to collections
To make good the three R's of wastes
Reuse, reduce and recycle
Towards creating thousands of jobs"

5. CLEANERS

Cleaning service job is very broad categorized under **AESTHETICS/ HELPING JOBS**. This is a **job** that would be relevant till eternity until man does not have any waste again. Personal hygiene for the baby to adult of all parts of the body from the head to the toes is a big task that needs some hands to help for a fee. The same applies to the taking care of the home, cars, kitchen and its utensils, cleaning and washing the carpets/rugs, upholstery, inner facility rooms like toilets, bathrooms and kitchens stores, premises (trimming of flowers, opening of the gutter/drainage, watering the flowers, pumping machine maintenance and supply of water to the tanks . . . You should know that **cleaning service** is one of the helping jobs even those who are not literate are in need especially car wash for commercial drivers. You are so important to the people and the society. A **Professor** needs waiters, maids, messengers, personal/research assistants, drivers/chauffeurs, chefs, librarians, typesetters, house-keepers, gatemen and many other domestic chores (house/office) workers as his occupation, situation or event calls for to be able to carry out his task effectively. In the category of workers, they are all workers that have the right to entitlements after certain years of meritorious service. Therefore, never see yourself as inferior. **Whatever you have interest to do, ensure it is done with passion.** The reward is the next to knock on your door sooner than later. Make some enquiries from cleaning service providers in big hospitals, schools . . . on the large number of workers on their payrolls; the worth of the cleaning contracts itself. You would know that **cleaning service** is a very big business than what you can imagine. In most cases, you are going to be provided with all the tools needed, only **your time, skills and efforts (strength)** are **to be paid for!** Those can be categorized under factory, office and home services!

> *"Cleanliness, they say, is next to Godliness*
> *Looking good is appearing neat and tidy*
> *And the environs including you become clean and green*
> *What you don't have time for*
> *Provide the needed tools for others*
> *Who would provide the service in a unique way*
> *Cleaning business is a big aesthetic business*
> *Inevitable to individuals, homes and offices"*

6. BEAUTIFICATION, COSTUMES AND FASHION

Every creature and creation looks beautiful with **aesthetics**. Sky with sun, moon and stars aside other planets as **aesthetics**. Residents and residential areas, business districts need look inviting through one form of **aesthetic** or the other. Cleaning and keeping the drainages and waterways are form of it. Events should also just as everything on earth. A beautiful environment has some **aesthetics** that make it so. Such includes landscaping, scenting flowers, trees that give shed and breeze, settees for relaxation, inviting lights at nights and some games station. Believe me, all your tools are either in your home or get provided by those who employ your time and skill. Write **good proposals** to residents/business districts associations to get started! A pretty damsel is always in the mind of an eligible bachelor. What makes things, environs (home, street, village, town . . .) beautiful and attracting? Costumes, of course! The costumes are the aesthetics that are appropriately applied by an expert for a fee. The provider/costumier is an innate and sometimes need little observation from those who are expert in doing it, just like decoration of events (events planning) with balloons and curtains of different colours and designs . . . Traditionally, girls are taught how to apply make-up (cosmetics), wrap/tie headgear, manicure and pedicure. The customers will pay for all the materials; you just need to be creative in the way you decorate to make the event venue glow with glamour. Ensure your first clients are your family members and those very close to you. Within short time, you will attain certain level of perfection. If you do that with passion, within a short period of time, you would get more clients and more money to create a big business. Sincerely yours, as a local trained girl, you understand these better than girls raised in the urban and the latter would no way need your service. Aside that, can you plait or weave hairs? Do you know how to braid hairs? The beauty to the hair through them would secure you a good earning if you can take it up as a **job**! It is an open-secret that they need you to look beautiful to get what they need (money, attention, love, closeness, from their spouses or male friends. There is no week you will not have more than expected customers on booking. Look, they cannot do that by themselves so that is why they call for your service, charge moderately. Make weekly saving to set up this business in an office. Dress for brides, sportsmen, celebrities, thespians, VIPs, occasions and get your perks. At the beginning, do home and mobile service till you are able to raise enough to start well. Do you understand the act of knitting? Some people prefer hand knitted cardigan for their children than those from machine for many reasons. They can choose colours of their choices and design how they want the products to look like. Some monotheist religions do not legislate and sanction modelling and certain modern facial, hair, limbs and skin treatment as legal **jobs.** Watch your limits! Therefore, all sorts of beautification like skin tattooing, fashion eyelashes, artificial fingernails, false hairs, teeth, nails ... are prohibited as these would debar the females, in particular, find most culprits, indulging in these to nullify their devotions. (watch out for '**Jobs for the Monotheists**' by the same author). In the book are details of choices of **jobs** for the Monotheists.

7. INTERPRETATION OF MESSAGES, BODY LANGUAGES, DREAMS, MYTHS AND IDEAS

Do you have the listening ears to understand other ethnics' dialects? If you are so endowed that you are bilingual or multilingual, then you have hit the goldmine. Turn this into economic benefit for corporate organizations and research institutes. Many institutions need someone who will help them market their products and services even if you do not study the relevant courses. What they are in dire need is the competent man for the **job** who translates their dream into a reality within a short target time! Never be surprised if you learn that your colleagues that passed out doing the same course has been employed by oil (exploration) company with huge package of remuneration serving as agent between the stakeholders, the company and the aborigines! This is a **job** from your natural ability! Oh the 'illiterates' (We mean those who are skilled/gifted in writing attractive proposals), can you summon courage and implore somebody to help you write an irresistible application to such organizations even the embassies? Sincerely yours, such who have such gift are rare and you should make something out of the knowledge freely endowed you.

> *"Ability to understand and speak others' dialects*
> *Interpreters are gifted and learned highly revered*
> *Schools, businesses . . . need your service just as individuals*
> *Worthy job enough to butter your bread both sides*
> *Starting from doing a service gratis*
> *And your knowledge spread to others like wild fire*
> *A well—packaged proposal with a connector suffice*
> *Suffice to land you a contract with target clients*
> *Hurry up to get a mouth-watering offer"*

8. MODELLING

Are you straight with good curve without body scar and pimples? Do you have clean skin? Look at the way you walk and talk (catwalk), do people appreciate you while walking and talking? What about your smile and cute answer to questions? What about your height, your muscular build-up (for men)? Do you always keep a smiling and inviting face? Believe me; companies need you for their adverts on billboards. Designers are looking for you in adverts placed on the print and electronic media. Get the information from browsers of internet. Spare time to watch shows on television and the reality shows. Once you are discovered and given an offer, sky is your starting point/benchmark. Do this; send your recent pictures as a model with application to model for the company's products or service and you will see the result. <u>This is not for the monotheists.</u> Therefore true devoted monotheists should stay away from this **job!** Read and pick yours from the title **"Jobs for the monotheists"**.

> *"In today's world of power of adverts*
> *Even in the world of entertainers*
> *Models, you are inevitable*
> *Nay, ye religious damsels!"*

9. MARKETING

Do you have the brains, multi-lingual, vocal and not a shy person? With this, you are very intelligent and brilliant. Somebody needs your contributions to their progress. The needy are the corporations and celebrities. Many manufacturing companies need those who could do personal selling for them on the streets, road . . .inside passenger buses, moving trains to publicise their products and services across the regions. Celebrities especially the politicians and the political office holders are in dire need of image-makers (publicist) who can be their spokesmen. Your professional skills and creativity/versatility matter in this dispensation. You can do this without paying a dime! This form of outdoor marketing is mostly used with mobile marketers and the minimum qualification is school certificate holders. Sometimes, you must understand the products/service/personality to be marketed or you are taught about the composition. Mind you, full—time housewives are your competitors as they can do the same **job** profitably right from their homes. (Make a booking for a copy of the title **"Housewives are prospective entrepreneurs"** by the same author). Alternatively, if you do not be an employee, hence dreaming to become independent marketer, with this as your focus in mind, you should be able to save enough money to start this highly lucrative business in a small scale. Sincerely yours, you have the chance of getting permanent **job** if you can speak some other dialects. That sets you apart from others. If you decide to take full employment as an employee, showcase your multi-lingual talent and you have invited the interest of the Marketing Managers, campaign director (for politicians/ parties) to repackage your remuneration. Learn and improve on your learning to understand major languages of the world to gain bigger market shares for greater commission as an independent/employed marketer. I tell you, if you understand **French, English, Spanish, Arabic, Chinese** and some advanced economies languages, you could become an international independent marketer/distributor, interpreter for diplomats, multilingual typesetter for publishers and film/script producers. Get me clear, for the local dialects that you understand, local factories need your service to boost their income, apply! Just **prepare and send your curriculum vitae to companies across the world through internet** and you will live to send kudos to this writer! In addition, you can market your acquired skills learnt in the course of learning at school to those who can afford to pay for your service. Take for instance, if you are good in using Microsoft Words and Corel Draw, many typesetting/secretarial offices are in need of your service likewise corporations and individuals.(Get a copy of JOBS WITH ZERO CAPITAL VOL.2 to add pep to your understanding and exposure to **new jobs**)

> *"Marketing service precedes production and selling*
> *It comes before you produce the product*
> *Or even package the service*
> *In term of limitations, so broad is the scope*
> *Much you have learnt from above*
> *To start with zero-capital with your skills and talents*
> *Including your qualifications*
> *Move out to get a good link/broker!"*

10. **NATURAL TALENTS**

In nation of millions of geniuses and many academic institutions that open their brains to the reality and challenge of time, innate talents of individuals if maximised, well nurtured and packaged, would surely create more **jobs** than the combination of the existing private companies and all government **MDA's** can provide. Maximising talents, skills and abilities **add value to lives** of people here (within the shores) and there (outside the shores).If truly **one out every five is a black and a Nigerian** and **two out of those five is a genius** according to study, then, **Nigeria, with about 167 millions (as at 2011) the cradle of black civilization**, can boast of having millions of natural geniuses in all fields of specializations. The talented ones in different fields are these and **a talent can provide jobs for at least ten direct and indirect workers at the initial stage (small scale)**. It shows that millions of the populace will be gainfully employed. Middle income earners will be so enormous that per capita income would have increased to the anticipated level of **Human Development Index of the United Nations**. Religions beliefs matter in choosing to develop any talent. It is advisable for a talented person to consult the priests before he/she start to develop skills in a particular talent. According to studies, **a nation that does not have middle income earners is in abject poverty.** In short, these talents can provide basic needs for about eighty millions directly and indirectly. Within some space of time if such talents grow bigger (medium scale) to accommodate more workers, the ability to employment more than

seventy percent of the populace is there whereas not all the people have to work to live a decent live. Some would be dependants. Some would do volunteer **jobs,** some would be government employees. Some are for research institutes and foreign organizations. The excess **jobs** would be taken up by immigrants from other nations! We have discovered numerous talents that people can work on to be self-employed without investing a dime. Let us talk on some of these **talents** as they **pave way to jobs with zero capital:**

a) **Bilingual or multilingual**

Do you know of rare people who read, listen to radio and watching television at the same time? If you are a type that easily understand other people's language (reading and writing), then you are never jobless as what you need is to showcase this rare talent at all or choice events. Someone will pick you up and package you for big corporation. Publishers need you home and abroad to transliterate some of the books to other dialects which you are so blessed. Broadcasting houses (print or electronic), local and international financial institutions, schools (colleges), communication networks providers, Non-Government Organisations, government **M**inistries, **D**epartments and **A**gencies, consultants, manufacturers and many others need your service! You have a greater advantage if you can typeset in major foreign languages. This gives you room to fix your price (remuneration)! Send your curriculum vitae and attached all the necessary documents/samples of evidences that are relevant to them. Walk from office to office of your choice industry/ corporation and drop your resume locally. Send the rest through mails and e-mails to others outside your walking coverage from your save from social fund. Film producers also need your service for subtitling their movies and documentaries. You have been blessed with a rare talent that would make you dine and wine with the top echelons in business worldwide. You will be an interpreter or at best a Consultant for **D**iplomats, **C**hief **E**xecutives **O**fficers of international businesses, **P**residents, **G**overnors, **K**ings, **Q**ueens, **M**inisters, celebrated sportsmen, artistes, **R**eligious/public figures, research assistants, librarian/ library assistants . . . and at best becoming an outstanding **S**ales **B**roker/**C**onsultants if you really package and present yourself to the right market and people. This ability can help you develop skills in reading hence become a compere of repute for social parties/gatherings (Religion, sports, entertainment, socio-economic, political . . .). This is a one-man show, another talent you can start doing without investing a dime in terms of money except your moral uprightness. Start from reading for pupils in schools, then to audience in seminars, symposia, gatherings, ceremonies and all social events. People pay to listen to a good, vocal and charismatic reader. In this clime, such is sprayed with mints though illegal! Come out of your shell and mix with the right environment where your talent will be appreciated and paid for!

b) **Drawing**

Drawing as **an art** is a must material for publishing houses. Books, especially children's books, must have graphic illustrations. Just imagine the market share of children in the world. One can say that the population of children is the largest even in the poor nations as the birth rate is always high. It shows that books for children in form of cartoons and those in animation for kiddies show on electronic media cannot do without the works of an artist. Print media (newspapers, journal, magazines . . .) need works of art to add spice to their production. Aside the cartoon section to pass some sensitive information or social stories, some are done to write a full serial story! Textile and printing industries need your talent. An innate talented artist who has the knowledge of drawing and painting only needs to design a good resume, add some of his/her works already on waste sheets or a drawing book, then send to textile factories, newspaper/magazine/comics/entertainment/books/ journals publishing houses and related organization for patronage. Schools adopt subject of art to make **self-reliant graduates.** Such graduates of arts are trained to be boss of themselves! Houses, banks, schools, cinemas, event centres, halls hospitals, offices . . .even the streets need works of arts on display to add to the aesthetics and to pass vital information (e.g. creation of awareness of non-government Organisations' programmes/messages on walls). In short, expose your talents to those mentioned examples of users and follow the guides in this book as earlier enumerated. Once your family or corporation or institution or social organisation is happy to display your beautiful works of art, others will soon join the league of clients for the business to grow. Get a drawing book and a pencil, start drawing on a piece of paper (not necessary a drawing book) on choice issues. Ensure you draw to inspire and to translate ideas and thought of your target clients. Choose the target users as your first focus. Ask yourself "<u>Who am I drawing for?</u> Is it for the children or the adult, the corporate organizations or public, local people or foreigners, Schools or hotels . . . ? Someone will sell and broadcast your talents to the world for patronage watch out! In the second part of this work are unique and highly lucrative works drawing would lead you to.

c) **Painting**

Painting, as an aspect of **art**, is vastly becoming one of the aesthetics in corporate organizations, houses, hotels, schools and institutions. Painting inspires as it passes message to viewers who can cudgel their brains. It could be on the past, present and projects the future. A naturally endowed should use his certificate from other discipline to build prospect in nurturing this innate talent. There are exhibitions across the world where arts are celebrated and appreciated. Works of arts are auctioned and could fetch the owner fortune that such cannot acquire in many years under another person's or company's appointment. Numerous are painters of visual arts that have won national awards and international recognitions through their works. Start small from getting some crayons and later grow to the use of brush on drawing books. The materials are affordable from a little saving from your meagre social fund! Selling a few works on display to your first set of clients according to this work would fetch you some money to grow bigger in a small space of time. The first sale could be so small, but take that to nurture the other works you have! To be a man is not a day **job** besides **Rome** is not built in a day! (Read more in another title from the same author titled 'waste to wealth jobs')

d **Writing**

The scriptures say ***"He who taught (the use of) pen taught man that which he knew not"***. Writers are dreamers and the inspired whose thoughts always turn into reality. It is the first thing to do before any invention. Government policies, political and economic, are written down before implementation. Film makers produce the scripts and these guide the actors and the actresses to play their roles. People forget what they hear easily. When they forget, they pick up the book. The songs being listening to today are first composed and written in books. Even the scriptures are written in books for access to the Divine information (manuals) therein! Most of the writers study the environment (air, seas, crusts and the features and creatures in and on them), they ruminate, days and nights, about the events (past and present) and try to proffer solutions to the problem in the society or forecast the future. They are inspired by events. Some learn in dreams. They listen to views and comments. They dream of the reality. It is believed that the secrets of the heavens and the earth are in the books especially the scriptures. Writing is an inspiration and sometimes revelations and the gifted writers is 'the pen of The Creator'. What do you write to make money? You can write stories for all the categories/classes of the people in the society. Stories for the nursing mothers on parenting; for children to teach traditions and morals with their language and simple style; to burn desire for research for the scientists; to solve economic and political crises; stories of the past hero and heroines; and stories for motivation and inspiration . . . Such can be for film producers as in script writing. What a writer writes is scripted for an actor/actress to act in films/documentaries. You can develop this **act and art** of writing into writing songs (read more in the next volume), jingles, adverts for companies, individuals and social/political engagements, Screenplay also brings in fame and fortune. If you have natural interest in writing any of the literary genres you specialize in (poetry, prose, play, playlet, children literatures . . .), fiction (dream/imagine) and non-fiction (real—life), start writing and sky is your benchmark! Believe me, in today's technology in publishing where a story is sold online across the world, a story can make you a millionaire overnight as it can be produced in form of **e-book, Mbook, paperback** and converted into script/ audio book/drama for movies wherein you will have all the rights **(100%)** for the **copyrights!** Think of audio-books, animation/ cartoon books (that can even attract the electronic media houses for the kiddies hours) audio-visual book (that can be played in cars and laptops/palmtops wherein reading is on a side and the act of the page on the other side of the screen).Imagine your book becoming **a best-seller** and the expected windfalls wisely invested in blue chips! This writer at the initial stage before he sold another title to publish another title, took off from writing on waste sheets of papers, used some amount from his feeding expenses from a low-earning **job** to typeset and then forged ahead with the use of little contributions from three friends who believed in his talent to start his self-publishing business. In fact, he is doing this for fortune and fame. Recall that he started from self-publishing after realizing his natural potential which today has some books on the list of the international publisher in **United Kingdom** and **United States** . . . His certificate on **Business Administration** has been a tremendous value as it adds values and spices to his natural talent (writing) and his hobbies (researching and travelling). Let there be symbiosis of what you learnt from the four walls of the classrooms and your talent provide you a lucrative **job** instead of staying idle and else wasting away invaluable time!

N. B. Never allow sweet tongues of a promoter, publisher, producer, director or marketer make you to leave your work without instant payment even a piecemeal to invest on another work, you are liable to be duped! If you are a commissioned writer, make sure you get part-payment before you start the work at all, in the middle point as funds needed to finish the **job** and the last payment before you leave the **job** for the owner as sometimes situation makes some stonehearted men to be untrustworthy and dupers! This writer is admonishing you from personal work experience. Surely, you will get patronage for your efforts. (Contact this writer on how (guides) to sell your talents on +234 803 2155 018, +234 805 6710 944 or latlib222@yahoo.com for free guides)

e) **Acting**

Do you crack jokes for amusement and people often enjoy them? Comedy, as all other parts, in play is a monetary rewarding act. They are parts of **arts**. The way some people dress, talk, walk . . . use their eyes, nose, ears, buttock . . . is a source of amusement to people at leisure period. Package the one you have and mix with those who make their livelihood from it as mentors. They will discover you and lift you up, polish your raw talent, assign you role and sell you to the audience for a good price. Remember, the stars of today come to stardom from collecting peanuts. Those who act for million today once collected stipends for the early appearances, so never be discouraged with your first disappointment. Some even appeared on stage and studios gratis. If you discover that you have the natural ability to act, then do not waste time to come out of your shell!

f) **Dancing**

Dancing is **an art** that one can inherit or get trained for formally and informally. Starting from understanding the traditional dances, perfect them and start to learn foreign dances. Dancers are employed into all states cultural troupes and singers also recruit them for shows. Business organizations also pay for their services for their promotions not to talk of the politicians especially in the tropical part of **West Africa.** As songs inspires so also dances inspires. Dance tells of an ethnic group. It speaks of culture and reminds people of their roots. The larger the number of the ethnics (in a nation), the larger the types of dances we have. Most ethnic groups can boast of not less than five different types of dances. In fact, the more the number of singing instruments in a locality, the more the number of dances there. Drum beats give the direction to the dance. Dance drama passes priceless message to an intelligent audience who can decode such dance. It is a form of amusement that not many people are so endowed. People can pay money to watch dances (ethnic, dance drama, festival) alone especially schools, business organizations, government . . . as a form of amusement. Choreographers are paid to train people how to dance in films, shows, events which is to show that your natural art of dancing is worthy of developing to make you a star artist! Mind you, the traditional dresses from your wardrobe and your natural skills on dancing are the major tools you need aside the efforts to locate a theatre or a troupe. Sometimes, the dancing troupe or the theatre group provides all the costumes! You can make names from being a one-man dramatist/dancer with the use of your idle, outdated, undersize and oversize clothes inside your wardrobe including your costumes!

g) **Singing**

Singing is an **art** just like other talents. Someone who is endowed with good, attractive and audible voices could be nurtured to become a commercial and renowned singer. There are some in the above category that cannot write songs. Meanwhile, poems are part of songs. A composer or writer of songs/poems needs a singer/reciter to make his work commercially viable. The latter should know that as you write books on all facets of human and animal lives, so also you should be flexible to write songs that touch and transform lives of people. It is recommended to write love songs, advocacy songs, traditional songs/poems, gospel songs (of your faith) as inspirational songs enrich living. This reminds me of a songs/poems buyer in **United Kingdom.** Just visit website and search for songs buyers/producers across **Europe** and you will have more than your expectation. Your singing talent should not be left to die with you. You need to sell yourself at the right market. Remember you can sing at events of different organizations, for film makers, for soap operas, for advertisers and advertising agencies, political gatherings, students on campus and at parties! Your position in the entertaining industry is inevitable especially if you can still compose songs or poems that suit such occasion. To start with, you can become a solo singer or poem recite (a one-man band) for audience and have the chance of been successful in it like the **Dan Marayas of Jos, North central of Nigeria and many solo singers in the world**. Your self—packaging matters in this case. Remember that if you want to reach the highest, you have to start from the scratch. Be contented with the little offers you as a rising star, you will reap in manifold when you become a superstar. Pick up this challenge and make a giant and right step at this right time!

h) **Drumming**

Drumming as an art complements a singer's tunes to make the venue more charged. Some who traditionally inherited the art should not leave the art to die a natural death. Most singers in the world use drums and other modern instruments to back-up their act. Ethnics are blessed with different drums with different drum beats that induce dancing away sorrows at parties and social events even at the rallies of the politicians in **Africa.** A party where songs and beats are not readily available is always dull. In most cases, spectators at open shows and theatre pay to watch the display of all the members of the band and not the singer alone. Playing at shows is seen as a team work just like the players in the football pitch. Those with this rare talent should sit down to work out things or see a music counselor/promoter for engagement. For those who do not have western education, they use their own education(innate/inherited knowledge in understanding the in and out of drums and drumming to train others and at best be an uninvited guest and player at a selective social events where someone could pick him, up for nurturing and connection. You are the salt in all events just package yourself well. Remember the inputs.

i) **Speech-making**

This is also an art. One can attest to this in any public function. **Ensure you read wide to improve your speech value.** When a bad speaker is speaking, the audience sleeps or loses concentration. Give the microphone to an orator and charismatic speaker, the whole venue become so charged and concentrated that at intervals they will give the speaker standing ovation. Such is a motivational speaker by nature. Such should be a bookish. These people who are so talented in speech making are fit into Public Relation Officer of a company, individual or agency. At social events (birthdays, naming ceremonies, funerals, graduation ceremonies, political rallies, launchings, luncheons, Annual General Meetings,

Symposia, Workshops), they serve as moderators/facilitators/master of ceremony/compere. If you are so talented, start advertising yourself for your people (individuals, companies, agencies, voluntary organizations . . .) to give you a chance. You can start from **free job** where you will introduce yourself to guests and give out business cards done from your nest egg to special/selected guests before you leave the stage. If you are at your very best at the event where your introduction was made, expect big patronage with cash, later with a ride! Again, can listeners pick your words while speaking? Do you see joy and concentration to you while speaking? Are you also versatile in the command and use of languages? Can you read the minds of your audience and give them what they need? Are you flexible in the use of ethnics' dialects to carry along your audience? Can you speak to change the mood of your listeners at any point in time? If your answers are **"YES"**, then, you need not be looking for jobs but you need social network to get you hooked. Ensure you get the message of the venue and some other vital information about the events before you get there. This will help you to rehearse before your appearance. You can be equally employed by studio managers and freelance media practitioners for an agreed price (remuneration). I tell you, you need a manager/promoter to repackage your raw talent and present you to the world for acknowledgement!

j) **Recitation**

Can you recite poems written in your dialect? It is no doubt that not all people that are gifted in writing poems are so gifted in chanting them. A poem writer not so endowed needs a reader to the public who is the reciter. Such also reads varieties of books and learn a great deal about cultures. Many music promoters/producers need them in studios. Many film makers need them in their films as cast as appeared in the film scripts. Recitation of traditional poetry heals the sick and arouses feelings. Make sure you train your voice in way to suit each line of recitation. Traditional poems for every occasion should be researched for your use to be more commercially viable. Studios and theatres are in dire need of you, locate them! You are a good reader, read in public schools, seminars, workshops to make both money and fame.

k) **Art works**

This includes sculpturing and handiwork like weaving of palm fronds to make cane chairs and desks. Hotels, organizations, individuals who values interior aesthetics are around to patronize your products. They are in dire need of these interior decors but could not find the producers/sellers. You just need to be creative in all your designs to attract more clients for your products. Before you know it, you could be exporting the products to neighbouring towns and states including nations. Visit cyber cafes to add to your knowledge as per production and selling of your wares. **Social network** would ever boost the business as you will have people trooping in to your home-office showroom later. Start small and you will grow. You will get your materials free from farm owners with your good human relation to them likewise some sharpening tools.

l) **Sporting activities**

This is vast as far as sports and their dynamism are concerned. There are international sports that are universal and there are some that are traditional. The universal sports are the common sport activities to us namely football. swimming, athletics (running, jumping, throwing . . .)indoor sports like tennis(lawn tennis, table tennis, badminton, gymnastic, chess, scrabble),handball, volleyball, weightlifting, boxing, judo, golf, baseball . . . Each ethnic group has different traditional sports such as **'emu' or 'eke'**(local wrestling, kick boxing), **'ayo olopon'** (traditional 'draught')among the **Yorubas** in **Nigeria**! Many ethnic groups have their form of sports for relaxation and competitions to win a bride as a take away prize in some cases. Develop the one you are so endowed with and excel. Turn the local sports in your region/tribe into a big money spinning venture through modern repackaging! Think of using other people's money. Those who have the money are looking for a well packaged sports venture like that to add value to their wealth. Many made names in football. Many made their marks in the sands of time in boxing. Remember **Muhammad Ali (formerly Cassius Clay), undefeated Rocky Machianos, Sugar Ray Robinsons** in boxing. **Pete Sampras** and the **Rafael Nadals** in lawn tennis; **Michael Jackson** in singing; **Carl Lewis** in athletics . . . In fact, what the raves of the moment in these sports are doing with fame and wealth should spur you on. Each time you hear such names like **Cristiana Ronaldos, Lionel Messis, the Klitscho brothers, Usain Bolts** and the rest of them, they are **sports ambassadors** therefore you should pick up your acts and live up to something! **Do not allow this/these talent(s) to rot away! Your talent is enough to lift you to the podium of grace, hall of fame and honour,** dining and wining with the Presidents, Kings and Queens, receiving awards and encomiums, getting diplomatic passports and stay in any nation of your choice across the globe!. It will only cost you showing yourself at a sporting training arena and make it a routine to train with teams and individuals (coaches and players) till you are picked for a trial. If the trial comes to you on a platter of gold or by fate, make the best use of that opportunity as such might take longer time to come again. You can also register with an athletic agency for connection locally or through the internet. Let me tell you, you are the 'headache' of some of the trainers and scouts as they need your rare talent. Assuming you are a type that can use both legs to score in football, a trainer who is in dire need of that versatile player in you may have been trying many players since, but if you make yourself available at the training venue of the club and you train with them, the shirt automatically becomes yours and the remuneration attached! At such venues, you would be kitted eventually. **Remember the Ethiopians and the Kenyans who dominated the long distance races worldwide trained bare footed on mountains!**

"Three areas are money-spinning ventures today
Namely the religion, the entertainment and the sports
Tailor your developed and identified talents towards any
Fortunately, as you have philanthropists in religion homes
So also exists scouts and philanthropists in the other two

Aside many who intend making more money with their money (prospective investors)
Move into right arena to showcase what you have
Join troupes of same discipline
Show creativity and your ingenuity
Learn from others to refine your trade
Mind you, cultural/ religion beliefs play a great role
Heed the priests' scriptural guided limitations, oh you monotheists!
Avoid what yours abhor while preparing showcasing your talent
Muslims female voice is naked, hence such should find alternative to singing
Many religions prefer praise-singing the Creator, never mortal human beings
Choose to showcase your talent
After several impressions, you will hit it gold!"

OTHER JOBS WITH ZERO-CAPITAL (SUPPLEMENT)

A. Baby-sitting

This is a major and special **job** for nursing babies and toddlers on an agreed fee between the mum and nanny. It is common among couples who are under contract of employment. Time to nurse the babies/toddlers may not be enough and the reason for employing a baby-sitter. Feminism has made this **job** one of the major **jobs** in **Europe** and other parts of the globe, though it is prevalent in the former. In addition, '**aged-sitter**' (someone who takes hygienic care for the old for a fee) is becoming another source of income. In **Africa** here, it is what is not advertised that is not patronized. Try to place a board advertising that a baby-sitter is at the beck and call at the highbrow areas and expect calls. Your ability to communicate in **English,** aside your local dialect, and neat dress would be a great advantage. Let me whisper this to your ears, the chance of turning the **job** into a crèche and later **Montessori/nursery** school is bright. In addition, your knowledge is the art and act of nurturing babies would help you in having toy shops for kids, fun centres among other business later if you remain steadfast and dream ahead time. Imagine what income to your purse if you are a **professional nurse** and **multi-linguist baby sitter!** I have witnessed how a proprietor started with a baby sitting from her parlour/living room. Today, she has a group of schools! (Read more in 'How to run tuition free school' by the same author)

B) Part-time/full time cook/chef

Singles, bachelors and spinsters, need someone who could do that for them. It is a thing you prepare from your kitchen and serve at the offices and places of occupation. Just be up to date in the collection of different diets for different clients and ensure you practice the delicacies before you produce for them. Learn to know the cooking tricks than your competitors to beat them all! Commit your mistakes within your kitchen and correct yourself. Criticise yourself and let your close pals and outsiders assess your worth (cooking/bakery skills). Learn more from others. Listen to your rivals. Look for where to make the difference. Read widely and consult. Attend courses and seminars. Develop more interest in this skill. ***Learn more learnable skills in this interest/hobby***. This is a good and necessary inevitable preparation. Failure sometimes is a good path to pass. Sometimes you are engaged to serve at events to the guests from different ethnics, so *'always be prepared'* as the scout motto reads. Many corporations, **jobs** and offices, to enhance smooth operation, effectiveness and efficiency, need prompt service providers. If you are naturally good in cooking and bakery, you stand the chance of getting patronage. Also, your resume that is detailed showing you as a natural cook could win a good **job** even though in most cases, such position is not advertised. The art of brewing non-alcohols and non-intoxicants, cooking and bakery start from a kitchen put your talent into play. Rehearse and allow your acts to be criticized within (by your family/friend especially learn to know what your enemy said about your rehearse) before you 'rebrand' and sell to for audience outside for consumption. These count. You could end up becoming a chef to the **'Very Important Personalities!'** Strictly follow the guides learn so far.

C) Environmental sanitation

In most third world nations, that has been a social problem contributing largely to adverse effects of climate change. Everything, place, object and creatures need to be beautifying to attract living and investment. ***A healthy nation is said to be a wealthy nation***. This is achievable if cleanliness is a priority. Can you create space for private refuse points for residents in streets and markets? Then, can you manage the points to dispose the refuse at the due time? If yes, you have got a good **job** from environmental sanitation. Never worry about the refuse containers, your clients would provide them! Make a plan by starting with two points with some clients and watch the service and the result in some months. If you are successful, increase the points. Add sorting to your business in order to conserve the dumping place. Start selling the sorted materials to recycling firms within and without. Internet is so helpful to get you clients for the sorted materials.

D) **Private car park**:

Do you have a close place in your house, even if inherited, very close to the street, manufacturing company or industrial estate, open market or a mall? You could turn that into private car park for a fee. Apply your intellect to avoid security risks as you must be security conscious! Therefore design a guide to have all the relevant information about the vehicle and its owner before the contract is sealed. By so doing, you have helped to decongest the road. (Read more in another book titled **'Waste to wealth jobs'** by the same author, watch out and book copies in advance from the publisher or send your short message service (sms) to:**+234 803 2155 018, +234 805 6710 944** or mail to latlib222@yahoo.com)

E) **Collecting new techniques**:

Move from firm to firm to get the secret of performing certain task. A stay at a farm settlement would accord you the chance of acquiring some vital skills and information as an internal economies of scale. Make efforts to the needy firm and the idea is saleable for a fee. You have done part of the work of the companies' **R**esearch and **D**evelopment **D**epartment! This can be done from reading tomes of books **(secrets are in prints)** and surfing of internet. Develop time to reading different works to learn new tricks. I believe that you have gained so much from reading this book. **Turn what you read into a reality**. Some are paid readers, but spare time to read at length across all prints to enhance your level of mental development!

F) PHOTOGRAPHY:

Do you have a mobile set with camcorder, camera with memory card? Then, you can start taking shots/snaps on issues (sports, amusements, social problems, challenges and events) for prized contests, for daily/periodical newspapers/magazines, private television houses for a good fee! We call this **'Photo speaks'**. Imagine how much you could be making from developing interest in this trade. Most of the shots with your mobile phone should be printed with your nest egg. Read more in the book **'Wastes to wealth jobs'** from the same author. The companies do not employ you, you employ yourself hence you must do with passion and creatively. Think and set the ball rolling (business plan) on how to expand your business from starting from photo-shots exhibitions where you invite big shots in the society. Start small by organizing photo exhibitions to schools through the proprietors for a subscription fee!

G) WRITING:

This is broad as you have read in the book. Here, you could be writing lines for advertising firms, communication networks and the interior decorators that are into gifts (greeting cards). Just have a focus on the topic at a time! With your laptop and information and communication technology knowledge, write software on different specializations and organisations!

H) VIDEO-COVERAGE:

Many film, researchers and documentaries outfits need your work recorded with your mobile handset. Make sure you work on the prevalent issues. Package very attractive proposals from your nest egg and deliver them by hand to the target companies. Imagine your income!

I) DOMESTIC PETS BREEDER:

Breed the harmless (friendly) and ornamental vegetarian pets (even snails, birds) for commercial purpose within your premises. A little savings from your basic allowance just as a writer saves a little to get the writing materials is only needed to get the first opposite sex. Go for high breed types!

J) SELLING PATENT RIGHTS TO START YOURS:

This needs lengthy historical illustration/explanations. Learn from the **history of Toyota family of Japan. Sakichi** succeeded in inventing an **automatic loom.** He did so by introducing several important changes to those of the **Europeans** to create an edge which got to the market in **1924** as **Toyota type G.** His son, **Kiichiro** reached an important agreement with **Platt Brothers and company** for the **commercialization** of the automatic loom. He was paid **100,000 pounds ($25million today)** for the right to produce and sell only to other markets except **Japan, China** and **United States of America. This was the initial capital he spent to start Toyota automobile!** You will learn more of several practical life experiences in the work **'Wastes to wealth jobs'** by the same author.

K) Cattery owner:

This is a person who creates a place where cats are taking care of for a fee from the owner of the cat. This is a good **job** for many housewives in a reservation area.

L) Stenography:

This is a professional skill that is specially needed by the executives in performing in their official assignment. If you get the skill, just like a fast and versatile typesetter, what you need do is to submit applications to organizations in mind or get the best use of your social connections to get a placement on either a part—time or full—time basis.

M) **Realtor**:

This is meant for those who already have credit ratings with financial houses. It is a situation where they buy and repair houses at choice areas depending on many factors that would make such a success story. Locate one, price and get the finance from your bank that would cover the repairs to increase the value. Do not contract out all the work to cut cost of repairs. Then, after all the repairs you sell to clients and repay your loans to the bank. Other similar **jobs** include buying grounded auto from auctions with your financier support, repair and sell to make profits.

N) **Going-concern related jobs**:

Many businesses are closing shops for many reasons especially one-man businesses that are commercially viable location. The location is good for companies to be used as their sales outlets if you get in touch with them. You can turn that place to a departmental store. Some intend to close shop simply because of financial losses. Some maybe as a result of the loss of a partner. In the course of this research, I met an estate agent who was managing many properties but decided to seek for green pasture outside the shores. Another person took over the business from him on mutual gentleman agreement. In some cases, what the business that is about closing his/her business lack you have. For example the strength to travelling up and down to meet and supply clients. Can you take up the risk? Do you have the expertise knowledge to carry on and turn the business around? Do you have the passion to engage your mental and physical endowments? If yes, persuasive proposal followed with a good business agreement (Memorandum of Understanding) would do the magic without investing a dime! Mind you, the dying businesses (or even the dead ones) that need resuscitation are in all the sector of the economy and social life within your nation. Discover them!

PART TWO

PRICING. INCOME. TRANSFORMATION. BUSINESS PLAN.

As aforementioned, at the initial stage, price invites customers to have a taste of your product or service and can equally chase them away, so use penetrating price technique to win customers. Your quality product/service will draw them to you even if you gradually increase the price later. **Be customer-friendly** in your approach as you have many competitors in the market and some about to enter this same market!

The **clients-producer** relations help to determine your income. Your increasing number of clients can help get more market share beyond your business coverage if cordial relationship exists between you. Ensure you satisfy your customers by effectively employ the **marketing mix** of four P's namely: **Product, Promotion, Pricing and Place. One,** give them worth for their money from producing quality and unique products. **Two,** use appropriate and most effective promotion for your product to have good acceptability by the segmented customers, target and prospective. As concisely explained above, adopt a good pricing strategy to create good market share and ensure that the product or service of yours reach your clients at place of need at the right time.

In short, produce the **RIGHT PRODUCT/SERVICE,** for the **RIGHT PEOPLE/CUSTOMERS**, using the **RIGHT PROMOTION** with the **RIGHT PRICE** and to be delivered at the **RIGHT PLACE** to make **RIGHT CLIENTS BASE** and **RIGHT EARNINGS**.

By transformation, we mean forward and backward integration. A writer can move on to go into self publishing and make it a passionate **job.** Likewise, a script writer can delve into film/movie making with some promoters. **A dancer** can transform himself from **a one-man show** (a dramatic monologue) into forming a dance group. This should the dream of many talented people.

On business plan, according to the noblest among us that ever walked on the crust, he was quoted to have said *"There is no wisdom that surpasses good planning"*. Every person should **have a plan** even a full time housewife. This plan serves as a guide towards achieving what at a particular point in time. If such is not met, then check and balance applies for correction or reprove.

THE LAST WORDS

Entertain no fear to start with <u>zero capital but **zero equity**</u> and other ways told. *"Fear is a habit, so is defeat, anxiety, despair and happiness. Eliminate all these negative habits with two resolves 'I can' and 'I will'. Another maxim says: 'Champions know that there are no short cuts to the top. They climb the mountain one step at a time. Perseverance is the key".* Every big multinational corporation starts from an idea, innovation and strivings to make it big. Start small; with time and commitment, you will be reference point later.

Entrepreneurial theorists believe that creating something so unique help in producing new **jobs** in millions (Book in advance for a title: **"New Jobs from the existing jobs"**). Add that to your mental dictionary.

REFRESH

Let us share some guides to boost your chosen business. Assuming you are into event planning and catering services by hobby or interest and you desire to develop them into money-earning venture. Make an 'official' visit to some schools around your home, approach the authority with politeness and business mind, discuss your business with them, and let them see reasons why their patronage within their premises will do for all the stakeholders as a way to foster good relationship between the parents and the school management and the gains for the pupils. They will surely enter into an agreement with you. You would be in charge of their catering services and events planning for the special days for the pupils and the school staff. As time goes on, collect data about the birthdays of the pupils and the staff. Remind them of the birthday before the d-day and remind them of your service to bake the cakes and other confectioneries for them by text messages. You have simply become a unique caterer within your ambience. Do not be surprised that some of the families of the pupils and the staff would soon become your clients.

Congratulations for reading through the pages. Have you grabbed the message therein, '**be—your—own—boss**', do not look out for unavailable **jobs,** that is eating away your precious time. Develop the winning edges. Small difference in your performance can lead to large differences in your result. Make a u-turn before grey hairs tell you that time is no more in your side! (For business enquiry, contact this writer on **+234 803 2155 018, +234 8056 710 944** on SMS only or mail to latlib222@yahoo.com)

"Listen to this last but inevitable admonition, dear readers
Capital to set up a business is hard to find
Especially in this era of credit crunch
Except you want to be mortgaged by capitalists for life
Get capital from proceeds of contests
Sell a patient right like **Kiichiro Toyota** *to start yours*
Employ all the OPM's taught to start your operation
Or sell a product/service raw to develop the rest
Sell a patent right with market limitation to start or even an asset
Employ the service of a broker/agent to get started
Enter into priced contests to get little capital
A few free seminars/symposia/shows/exhibitions could become a source of capital
Not forgetting a partnership deal and your personal savings as **nest egg**
And a client is ready to pay you in advance for the skills
All these are a worthy source to start small or big
Without resolving to go borrowing from your credit ratings
While setting up, think about starting small with the little with you
Avoid capitalists who dictate your business action line
Being—your—own—boss only takes some time and dedication
Not excluding both your moral and financial discipline
Follow the content to the latter
In addition, always prove your onions, be creative and versatile
Never mind the first peanut offer for your service and first product
Employ 'bootstrapping', sell some and re-invest the whole money
Make savings to expand your business or improve your service packaging
Big offer would soon come knocking at your doorstep and luck smiles at you
Just as a seed grows to become multiple-branched fruit-bearing tree
A small idea of yours would soon turn into big venture with branches
Most successful billionaires started with either a little or nothing
Join the league but master your craft along the path!
'A journey of one thousand miles starts with a step' Confucius said as reported
And if you can present persuasive proposal to a dying business
Showing your interest in the going—concern of such business
Good memorandum of understanding could follow such
And you have become employed as you retain others about losing jobs
Best of luck if you can!"

DO'S AND DON'TS OF A PERSUASIVE PROPOSAL

We have talked a lot the usefulness of persuasive proposal in most of the jobs introduced especially those that involve the established relevant firms. Someone whose work cannot be done at piecemeal needs to have the knowledge to write and deliver persuasive proposals to get promotion of his works under different categories aforementioned. Surf internet to update the content of your proposal and you make comparism with some other proposals. It is not bad if you give it to someone else to proofread and make necessary corrections, alterations, suggestions and recommendations after writing the sketch! Remember that Nobel laureates **Wole Soyinkas** of this world have their own editors! Treating winning proposal is outside this work but read about a few hints about a winning proposal to get your work see the limelight. They are:

1) *Start from showing interest in the problem of the business. After the proper/concise contact and mobile addresses with date to the right office, never write "Proposal to . . . ." or "Proposal on . . ." Rather state the problem as the heading like "Supplying of unique instructional materials on Mathematics"; "Unique research—based and potential award winning traditional story ready for sale"; Strategy to increase your sales and hence improve income".*

2) *Show the gains derivable for the business in the first paragraph. Reader has no precious time to waste. He/she is interested on something that can*

change their own business misfortunes or improve their goodwill/income. Do not write/compose irrelevant and never use foreign technical words or vocabularies. Write in paragraphs with relevant sub-topics. Bold and underline words that are necessary for purpose of emphases.

3) Show concise objectives and the target goals by new managers if you propose to take over a business or the key content of the story or package you are selling to the company/individual and not your own gains in mind. The promoter/owner intending to transfer his/her business does not care about you but him/herself. Men are selfish creatures. The latter does not want his/her legacy to ruin in his/her lifetime so you are needed to save edifice from crumbling and the former is in dire need of what could boost his/her earnings.

4) Show the intended outcome as benefits to the owner (goodwill and income) and people. This is a major goal to both of you. This is what the promoter/owner will gain from doing business with you. Do not beat about the bush or speak with your tongue in the cheek!

5) Show/attach your required resume and experiences and probably your partners to form the team of new owners if requested. A brief profile about you would show in your letterhead. Therefore, use an informative letterhead that speaks volume about you and your capabilities.

6) Show endorsement letters from guarantors/referees. This is a guarantee to win the hearts of the recipients of your proposal. People like to deal with someone with integrity and good reputation.

7) Show the facility at hand (could be other people's material (under your custody) to make the business wear a new look. Sometimes, what you are in possession of are the major need to resuscitate the dying or the dead business, prove to the owner that you have them! For a promoter hoping to adopt your work, show him/her the stuff that the work worths investing upon and the market potentials (acceptability).

8) Other relevant information asked to be supplied should be in the proposal. Imagine all other relevant information that should be there when you rob minds with those in the field before you. Sometimes proposals demand

the experts you are working with and the working experience. Some demand for certain estimates, supply them but be moderate.

N.B. Proposals vary in writing and presentation (content). Some need pre-proposal before you repackage it as a booklet. Technical ones require technical terms yet such should be unambiguous. Some may need budgets and estimates as prerequisite. Just write thinking about the receiver's need than your own target/need/gain!

However, in all the information being given, you have to be concise, truthful, show confidence, humble and use clear language.

ABOUT THE AUTHOR

This **gifted motivational speaker, socio-economic researcher, essayist, playwright, poet, child educationist, public, football and economic analyst**, is an alumnus of "**The citadel of Technological innovation**"-The Polytechnic, Ibadan, Nigeria with specialisation in **Business Administration and Management**. He is Computer literate and a prolific, naturally talented creative writer and researcher with **Addin Resources Ventures**, Ibadan, Nigeria. A product of **Bishop Onabanjo High School, New Bodija, Ibadan**, his alma mater where he was a **prefect** and a **winner** of a national essay for secondary schools. He is a native of **Ibadan**, by birth and an indigene of **Ogbomosho** from **Alapa royal family** by paternal parentage. To his credits are numerous published works in **Oyo State Ministry of Education** lists. One of which is a 'be—your—own—boss' prose series titled "**The Young Billionaires**", a preamble of the title "**Oasis**".